Oh My God!

Julie Aspinall

Oh My God!

The Biography of Chantelle

JB

JOHN BLAKE

Published by John Blake Publishing Ltd,
3 Bramber Court, 2 Bramber Road,
London W14 9PB, England

www.blake.co.uk

First published in hardback in 2006

ISBN-13: 978 1 84454 317 5
ISBN-10: 1 84454 317 X

British Library Cataloguing-in-Publication Data:

A catalogue record for this book is available from the British Library.

Design by www.envydesign.co.uk

Printed in Great Britain by Creative Print and Design, Wales

1 3 5 7 9 10 8 6 4 2

Papers used by John Blake Publishing are natural, recyclable products
made from wood grown in sustainable forests. The manufacturing processes
conform to the environmental regulations of the country of origin.

Every attempt has been made to contact the relevant copyright-holders,
but some were unobtainable. We would be grateful if the appropriate
people could contact us.

Contents

1	CHANTELLE WHO?	1
2	THE HEAT IS ON	23
3	MAD ABOUT THE GIRL	43
4	JIM'LL FIX IT	65
5	WILL THEY, WON'T THEY?	89
6	HE'S NOT MY PARTNER	113
7	THERE WERE THREE OF US IN THE RELATIONSHIP…	135
8	HOW IT ALL BEGAN	157
9	FAMOUS AND LOVING IT	179
10	THE BEAT GOES ON	201
11	THE PERFECT COUPLE	223
12	INTO THE FUTURE	231

1

Chantelle Who?

The nation was, as ever, agog. The latest series of *Celebrity Big Brother* was about to kick off and, scheduled to last three weeks, it was to be the longest the celebrity household was to be together so far. It had already attracted a fair share of controversy with the news that Michael Barrymore would appear in the programme. Once the darling of popular television, Barrymore had all but been living in exile in New Zealand after his career had gone into freefall several years earlier following a dreadful tragedy at his Essex mansion, which has never been entirely resolved.

Nor was Barrymore the only controversial choice of contestant: Faria Alam, the siren of the Football

Association, who had had an affair with, among others, Sven-Goran Eriksson, was also going to be in the house. Then there was George Galloway, the MP who had openly defended Saddam Hussein; Pete Burns, a singer whose appearance had become so bizarre he looked like neither a man nor a woman; and the actress Rula Lenska, who had been quite open about why she was taking part: the money. It was a line-up that seemed certain to produce sparks.

And, as ever, *Celebrity Big Brother* had been the object of intense speculation over the previous weeks. Like its counterpart *I'm A Celebrity... Get Me Out Of Here!*, it attracted both the very famous and the barely known. Also like *I'm A Celebrity...*, it carried the chance of career rejuvenation for those who had been spending more time than they would like out of the limelight, as well as offering more controversial figures the chance to show their real personalities. These two criteria applied most obviously to Barrymore and Galloway, but the rest of the line-up was promising too: Rula and, to a lesser extent, Pete were still widely known to the British public, as were Traci Bingham and Dennis Rodman, but more about them later. With the addition of a couple of lesser names, it was a good mix.

But on the night in question, 5 January 2006, a nation that was still slightly glazed after the recent Christmas and New Year celebrations was bemused to find that the first entrant into the house was not quite as well known as her fellow contestants. Indeed, no one had ever heard of her, for the simple reason that she wasn't famous. You could almost hear the chant rising from the nation's sitting rooms. Chantelle who?

For this year *Celebrity Big Brother* was kicking off with a twist. It was to include an unknown member of the public, who would try to convince the celebrities present that she, too, was famous. And so Chantelle Houghton, a 22-year-old blonde from Essex, who was described as a model promoter, was placed inside the house. Chantelle confessed that she was afraid of snakes and spiders, still lived with her mother and liked the colour pink. The public was to find out a great deal more about her over the coming weeks, but that was all that was known at the start. Her appearance on the show was not praised in all quarters, however. 'This idea is up there with some of the least entertaining ideas in *BB* history,' one critic said. How wrong that was to prove to be. Over the next three weeks, not only did Chantelle carry off her role to perfection, but she also turned herself into a genuine celebrity in the process. This was to be the most successful *Celebrity Big Brother* to date.

But that was all to come. Back then at the beginning of it all, Chantelle did have some kind of past to tell her housemates about, albeit an entirely imaginary one. In an effort to convince them that she deserved to be there, Chantelle was said to be a member of the pop group Kandyfloss, whose biggest hit was 'I Want It Right Now'. From the very start, the public was in on the secret, knowing that, if Chantelle managed to convince the others that she was who she said she was, she would be allowed to stay in the house. If they sussed her out, she was going to be evicted. The public perception, though, had it that there wasn't a chance of her winning. A non-celebrity winning *Celebrity Big Brother*? Even in the modern world, where people are famous just for being famous, surely that was an irony too far.

And so, under the guidance of Davina McCall, the contestants began the ritual march into the house, which was equipped with single beds, a gym and an outdoor pool. Chantelle, who had been named after a word her parents heard in Belgium, went in first, followed by Michael Barrymore, who was accorded a hero's return by the crowds waiting outside. Indeed, the 53-year-old entertainer was nearly in tears at the warmth of his reception and could barely tear himself away from his adoring audience, finally having to be escorted into the house by a crew member.

There he met Chantelle. Not that he was capable of taking her presence in at the time: there had been real fears as to how he would be received by the crowd but they couldn't have made their welcome any warmer. There were and are huge swathes of British society that want nothing to do with Barrymore, but they were not in evidence that night. 'That was too much,' he said. 'It was unbelievable. I'm shaking.'

Perhaps not knowing that Barrymore was a recovering alcoholic, Chantelle offered him a glass of wine, which he declined. He himself appeared to have decidedly mixed feelings about why he was appearing on the show. 'If people want to call it a comeback, they can call it a comeback, but I haven't been away,' he said before he went in, while Essex Police also made it known that they would be taking a keen interest in the show. For there were still many unanswered questions over the tragic death of Stuart Lubbock in Barrymore's swimming pool and they clearly felt that he might be able to recall more details on the show about what had happened that night. The atmosphere of the *Big Brother* household was strange, and more than one celeb and non-celeb alike had been affected by the combination of complete isolation from the outside world, rivalry to win the game, alcoholic overindulgence and sheer exhibitionism.

Next into the house was Pete Burns, the lead singer with the 1980s band Dead Or Alive. Pete was an unusual creature: while he made no attempt to modulate his voice to the tones of a woman, plastic surgery had given him a female physique and a feminine pout. Dressed in a long coat trimmed with fur, high heels and lipstick, he tottered into the house, announcing, 'I feel like I've been fired out of a cannon,' before adding to Barrymore, 'I know who you are.' Chantelle was not addressed.

There was an early warning about what was to come from him: 'I don't have team spirit,' he said. 'I play for myself.' He was to prove that and then some. Pete had an acid tongue which put him into a league of his own and sharply divided public opinion about him. Some people adored his excoriating wit; some simply couldn't take the harshness of his judgements on others. But, in a house rife with egotism and self-satisfaction, Pete was to prove more than capable of holding his own.

And so the march went on. Traci Bingham from *Baywatch* was the fourth housemate: she announced that she 'might have issues' in the house as she slept naked and wore no knickers. The vegetarian then added, 'I'm kind of a freak,' and admitted she'd had Botox and flirted with animals. Her interests apparently included fitness, interior design, meditation and gardening. Like Chantelle, her favourite colour was pink. How, she was asked, did she rate herself on a scale of attractiveness? 'Ten out of ten,' she replied.

After that, they swarmed in thick and fast. The rapper Maggot entered, to be asked by Chantelle whether his name was Maggot or Maggots. 'Maggot,' he replied, before having to tell Pete Burns who he was. Wild he was not: Maggot was to be one of the few people in the house who managed to remain calm and didn't try to force his will on everyone else. Then the actress Rula Lenska appeared and embarked on a round of double-cheek kissing of her fellow contestants. She was to 'broaden people's horizons as to who I am – a crazy Polish countess who likes a challenge'.

Next was the glamour model Jodie Marsh, who was to have the worst time of it in the house, and, indeed, there was a hint of the trouble to come in her opening remarks. 'I'm a famous author,' she said. 'I just want to be liked. I just want to walk down the street without somebody shouting abuse at me.' She then announced that people think she is stupid, thick, a slapper and a bimbo, before continuing, 'Apart from being stupid, I'm probably all of those things. I've dreamed of being famous since I was about five years old and it's all I've ever wanted in life. Now I have got it, I hate it.' It was not the most auspicious of beginnings, and nor was nominating Peter Andre as her worst possible housemate 'because I hate his missus'. There was clearly trouble to come, although, at the very beginning, Jodie was actually given the best odds to win.

The next entrant caused a certain degree of excitement within the house itself: the American basketball legend Dennis Rodman. Forty-four-year-old Rodman bore the distinguishing features of being both a cross-dresser and an ex of Madonna's, and had Traci shrieking, 'It's Dennis Rodman! Oh, Dennis, give me love!'

'Get away from me, Traci,' said the gallant Rodman, as Davina informed viewers that he had spent the previous night partying at Stringfellows and for his stay in the house had packed extra-large condoms and no underwear. And what was to be the most difficult aspect of Dennis's residency? 'The hardest thing will be three weeks without sex. That's gonna suck,' he said.

It should be noted, incidentally, that a good deal of

what the housemates said as they made their entrance was to come back to haunt them. Dennis might have complained about the hardships of going without sex, but, while he was still in the house, his first wife came out to denounce him for being obsessed with sex to the extent that he could practically never turn it down. (His stay was to prove an exception to that rule.) Jodie wanted to expunge her image as a woman not possessing the strictest of morals, but actually made it worse. George Galloway wanted to engage a new and younger generation with politics, but he came across as appallingly patronising to the younger members of the household and wasn't allowed to broadcast a word about politics at all. And so it went on.

As so many had found before them, each housemate was to discover that he or she was not bigger than the game itself and that even seasoned old pros could be manipulated by the directors, producers and cameramen. Although their time in the house was to prove a resounding success for some members, most obviously Chantelle, that was certainly not to be the case for everyone. Yet what did emerge from the strange mix of celebrities was gripping television. Over the weeks to come, the nation would talk of little else.

There was a rather mixed response at the

appearance of the next contestant, Faria Alam, who had done so much to enliven proceedings at the FA. Greeted with both boos and cheers, she made her way rather quickly into the house. After that, there was Samuel Preston, aka Preston, the guitarist and singer with the Ordinary Boys. He was the 'voice of reason', he said, adding that his pet hate was people who felt they had to be 'wacky all the time'. 'If I go out first I will almost certainly kill myself,' he went on. His motivation for doing the show was simple: 'I'd rather do it and regret it than not do it and regret it.' As matters turned out, he was not to regret it at all.

And finally came George Galloway, another recipient of much booing and catcalling. At the door of the house he bellowed, 'Stop the War!' and made a peace sign – not that it did much to placate his detractors. There had been a fuss from the moment it was announced that he would be taking part. 'His position as an MP does not preclude him from being a housemate,' said Channel 4. 'He will not be allowed to use his time in the house as a political soapbox.' This, it later emerged, was news to Galloway, who had been planning on doing just that.

Once inside, he announced to his housemates, 'George Galloway. I'm a Member of Parliament,' and went on to tell Rula that they had friends in common.

Davina, meanwhile, explained to the crowd outside that the person he least wanted to see in the house was Tony Blair, because he didn't want to be responsible for the 'first-ever live throttling of a British Prime Minister'. His main loves were 'his daughter, sunbathing and sex', and Fidel Castro was 'the greatest man he had ever met'. And that was that. They were in the house and a tumultuous three weeks lay ahead.

Rather to everyone's surprise, given the fuss over some of the real celebrities, namely Barrymore, Galloway and Pete Burns, the person who was the subject of the most curiosity was none other than Chantelle. It took a certain amount of guts to do what she was doing and, besides, people were curious. Who was this blonde who had sprung out of nowhere? Was what she was doing somehow immoral or just a comment on our celebrity-obsessed times? And, above all, would she get away with it?

Indeed, such was the interest in Chantelle that almost immediately details about her background began to emerge. She had been born in Basildon Hospital in 1983 and there was a certain amount of amusement when it emerged that she worked as a Paris Hilton lookalike; and, in fact, the resemblance is remarkable. Nor has she had exactly a shy and retiring past. In 2003, when she was 19, Chantelle had been a regular at racetracks across the UK as part of a 'babe squad', a position she acquired courtesy of the readers of the magazine *Motor Cycle News*, which, incidentally, had often also featured Jodie Marsh. Many pictures of a scantily clad Chantelle draped across motorbikes then ensued, but, rather to everyone's surprise, she didn't make it to the London Motorcycle Show in 2005. 'Everyone who worked with her said she was a really lovely person and really bubbly,' said the magazine's Tom Rayner. 'When she didn't get into the babe squad last year, we wondered where she went. And now we know.'

It soon became clear that this was not Chantelle's first foray into the world of celebrity. There were those appearances as Paris Hilton, for which she earned up to £300 for four hours' work, and as whom she had been photographed, little dog included, by Alison Jackson, a photographer who specialised in lookalikes. And that wasn't all: she had auditioned the previous year for the sixth series of *Big Brother*, which is where the producers of *Celebrity Big Brother* had first caught sight of her.

Chantelle's appearance as a celebrity had clearly been in the pipeline for quite some time. And then there were the anodyne facts: she loved shopping, enjoyed the hula hoop as her only form of exercise, fancied Jonny Wilkinson and gave herself four out of ten for intelligence. There she was almost undoubtedly doing herself down. Chantelle is clearly no intellectual, but to have got as far as she has done aged 22 by relying solely on a certain amount of bravado is not the act of a dumb blonde.

The housemates, too, were becoming increasingly curious. Although they had followed the speculation in the press as much as anyone else, it hadn't been clear until the very last moment exactly who would be going in and so they were keen to suss one another out. No one was in much doubt as to who Barrymore was, but lesser names like Preston and Maggot didn't mean much at all. And then there was Chantelle herself. While she completely looked the part she was about to play, she was nevertheless an impostor, whose task was to fool a crowd of very savvy people into believing she was something she was not.

Preston, of all people, and George Galloway were the first to wonder if something funny was going on, after Chantelle made a slip and informed Preston that Kandyfloss's single had got to number 58 in the charts, having forgotten that she had already told Galloway it had done better than that. 'I haven't heard of that group,' a suspicious Preston told the MP and Faria Alam.

'She had one hit – it got to number 47,' protested Galloway.

'She told me 58,' Preston replied. 'You don't think she's a red herring? I've never heard of her. If she's just a struggling musician, then I'd feel bad for being paranoid.'

With that, the two sent Faria to ask Chantelle how well Kandyfloss's single had done in an attempt to catch her out. But no further drama ensued. Chantelle's secret was safe for now – not that she had realised that anyone doubted her. In fact, her real concern was someone else altogether. 'I have no problem faking it,' she told the Diary Room, 'but I go to the same clubs as Jodie Marsh, so I think she recognises me.' Luckily for the increasing number of Chantelle fans, she was wrong.

Funnily enough, Chantelle was also the first of the housemates to seem to be about to become embroiled in a romance – though with Dennis, not Preston. The two got on immediately and on the first night in the house spent hours chatting as they lolled on adjacent beds. Dennis went so far as to show Chantelle a selection of his tattoos and piercings, before rather ruining it all by getting all the facts about her wrong. After spending time in the Diary Room, he announced, 'They asked me who I was bonding with and

I'm like, well, she's white, she's from Brisbane, she's named Champagne...'

'I'm not from Brisbane, I'm from Essex and I'm Chantelle,' his rather indignant new friend cut in.

Of course, Chantelle was far from being the only object of curiosity. Ever since it had been announced that Michael Barrymore would be a housemate, there had been a great deal of speculation as to how he would cope with his incarceration. Sure enough, barely 24 hours into his stint, he was acting a little strangely: he got up in the middle of the night talking to himself, spent some time prodding a cactus and then tried to deface a picture of the Queen. 'Dennis said my snoring was so bad he couldn't sleep, so I thought I'd get up,' he said.

As for prodding the cactus, 'I was trying to get one of those prickly things off to turn it into a pen,' he explained. His behaviour towards Her Majesty's portrait was even more eccentric: after having a little more sleep, he spent some time examining the picture before trying to poke the eyes out with a lemon squeezer, an act that got him reprimanded for vandalism by Big Brother.

But it did nothing to diminish him in the eyes of a public who seemed ecstatic to see the fallen entertainer back on their screens again. Indeed, in a move that took everyone by surprise, he became the bookies' 3/1 favourite to win *Celebrity Big Brother*, odds prompted by the euphoric reaction he got on his entry into the house. 'The public reaction proved that Barrymore's star is still shining,' said Ladbrokes spokesman David Williams. 'We feared he might be damaged goods but the phones started ringing as soon as the show was over.'

And not everyone knew the background to his troubles. Barrymore had, of course, famously split from his wife Cheryl more than a decade earlier after announcing that he was gay, and, sadly, Cheryl died in 2005. Barrymore himself was a little circumspect about revealing the details, initially telling Traci, 'I was married for 18 years. She died last year.' Only later did he confess, 'We split before that.'

But, he said, the tumultuous events of the recent past had changed him as a personality. 'If you come through those moments when you lose you and you get you back, you're actually the better person for it and your work improves because of it,' he said. 'That's providing you come through it.' Nor was he ruling out even having a child with his partner Shaun Davis. Watching his friends' children grow up had given him enormous pleasure, he said. 'That isn't to say I wouldn't like to be a dad, but what do you do – do you adopt one?'

Galloway, for his part, was being sympathetic,

saying, 'You're a funny man, Michael, you'll be back. And you'll be back big.'

Of course, there was a rather more serious side to all this and it came in the person of Terry Lubbock, the father of Stuart Lubbock, who died in mysterious circumstances in Barrymore's pool during a party in 2001. He was disgusted by the whole proceedings. 'The man breezed in there as though butter wouldn't melt in his mouth,' he said. 'It's repulsive. Has he no shame? I've been trying to psych myself up for this for a few days, but watching him milk the crowd was harder than I thought. And I just hope that some of the contestants don't let him off the hook when it comes to talking about the night my boy died.'

And, given that drink and drugs were in evidence on the night of the party, it didn't help that Barrymore had entered the *Celebrity Big Brother* house to the strains of 'Without Me' by Eminem, a song that deals with mixing 'weed' with 'hard liquor' and has the line 'I just settled all my lawsuits'.

'It was sick and totally inappropriate,' said Terry. 'But nothing surprises me with Barrymore and Channel 4. It is almost as if those responsible picked the most inappropriate, hurtful song they could. Our son's memory is being ignored in the pursuit of entertainment. They have not shown the slightest respect to Stuart's family.'

On a much lighter note, Chantelle was continuing to provide a great deal of entertainment. Every new fact that came out about her was seized upon with joy by the press, who breathlessly informed readers what they had most recently found out about the mystery contestant. For a start, there was that job as a Paris Hilton lookalike, which prompted some hilarity when friends started talking about their nickname for Chantelle. 'People have been commenting on her likeness to Paris Hilton for years,' said one. 'We call her Paris Travelodge, because she is the Essex version of the real thing. She's a nice girl, if a bit ditzy. She just wants to be famous.'

Clearly, she did, and realised from the outset quite what an opportunity *Celebrity Big Brother* could offer her. Chantelle's attitude to the day job was becoming a little laissez-faire, resulting in her losing some lookalike work. 'She was booked to appear on a balcony in Windsor on Charles and Camilla's wedding day,' said Caroline Green of Susan Scott Lookalikes, which is based in London. 'She called us on the day, saying she had been out the night before and was in casualty. On the next day, she phoned saying she couldn't work because she had burned her face by frying chips.'

That was the end of Chantelle's association with

that agency, but she was soon on the books of Fake Faces. 'Chantelle is perfect as Paris,' said a spokesperson for the agency. 'She creates masses of attention whenever she is out shopping. She is a wonderful girl. She made an instant impression on us and we wish her all the best. I'm sure this show will be the making of her. Being a true celebrity has always been her aim.'

Of course, by now there was the very real possibility of Chantelle becoming known for herself, rather than for her resemblance to someone else. And it didn't stop there, for it emerged that she had also featured as a sexy Soccerette on the Sky show *Soccer AM*. 'There's a dollybird moment where one parades down the catwalk wearing a team's shirt,' said a Sky spokesman. 'She really enjoyed herself. She did a bit of a wiggle on the catwalk.' She had also been featured on the glamour website popstargirls.co.uk, as well as appearing as a Page 3 girl in the *Daily Star*. And she was even on a dating website, where the Chantelle image came across loud and strong, with her favourite things listed as 'fake tan, Lionel Richie, roses, wine and popcorn'. The girl was destined to go far, and now she was definitely on her way.

As these revelations came to the fore, interest didn't wane in her – far from it. The viewers couldn't get enough information about her, which, ironically, had the effect of turning her into what she had wanted to be all along – a celeb. It turned out that not only had she auditioned for *Big Brother* the previous year, but she had even made it through to the practice run, which was when Channel 4 realised that they could use her better elsewhere.

What has been crucial to Chantelle's success – and the reason why the producers put her on the show in the first place – is her looks and personality. She looks like a member of a girl band, or a young celebrity, or an Essex girl, or whatever you want to call her, with the result that it was easy for her to fool the housemates and to step into the role of a celebrity as soon as she exited the house. And her personality was perfect, too: bright, breezy and unconcerned. If there is a dark side to Chantelle, she has done a sensational job of hiding it. Pretty and lively, she lifted people's spirits and, because she was 'the girl next door', the public loved her. The producers of *Celebrity Big Brother* couldn't have chosen better for her role.

As more details about Chantelle herself emerged, so more became known about her family, too. Her father, Alan Houghton, 53, was a cab driver who was divorced from her mother, Vivien, and professed himself as surprised as anyone else when he found out what his daughter was up to. 'I was flicking through the channels when I saw Chantelle on the telly,' he revealed. 'I couldn't believe it. I had no idea she was going on the show, but I had a feeling for some time that she was up to something. She does look like Paris Hilton. When I've seen her sometimes, I just can't believe it.'

He had been equally unprepared for Chantelle's debut as a Page 3 girl. 'I coach a football team and I had no idea she was going to be in the paper until I came into the dressing room and the lads had pinned pictures from the *Daily Star* up,' he said. 'She's a great girl and I wish her all the best.'

Her mother was equally bemused by it all. 'I was watching when I was getting ready for work,' said Vivien. 'It's really weird. I was up late on that first night. I'm trying to get my head together. It's very exciting.'

It emerged that Chantelle had worked in a bank and an office, as well as doing a stint as a barmaid in her family's local pub in Wickford, the Duke. There were even murmurs that she had worked as a lap dancer.

Inevitably, ex-boyfriends began to turn up on the scene. One, James Robinson, now a 22-year-old plasterer, was a little cautious in conveying his memories of his increasingly famous ex. 'She's a lovely girl, but I couldn't trust her,' he said. 'She was always lying about what she was up to.'

But what she was up to now was in a whole new league. Her housemates were warming to her – most of them, anyway – and the nation was engrossed. After just 48 hours in the *Celebrity Big Brother* household, Chantelle was achieving the stardom she had always longer for. Not that she realised that yet. Cut off from the outside world with her fellow celebrities – and that term was becoming accurate – she still had a long way to go yet.

2

The Heat is On

As *Celebrity Big Brother* got under way, the distinctive personalities of the housemates soon began to show through. Another potential romance seemed to be in the making, this time between Rula Lenska, who had been married to the actor Dennis Waterman, and the maverick MP George Galloway, of the Respect Party, who was in the process of being divorced by his Palestinian wife, Amineh Abu-Zayyad.

The two had been indulging in some heavy-duty flirting, and Rula, the 57-year-old star of *Rock Follies*, among much else, got a little carried away in the Diary Room when she was asked if there were any contestants she would like to 'explore further'. 'Yes – George,' she replied. 'He is an intelligent, erudite man, whose eyes show remorse and care and a lot of goodness.' Later, she appeared a little sheepish about having got so carried away. 'A combination of alcohol and the strange atmosphere of the Diary Room had rather loosened my inhibitions,' she explained. 'It makes you feel more relaxed in there,' she went on. 'It's like you suddenly have a voice. It's very bizarre.'

Elsewhere, the proceedings were rather less high-minded. Doubtless remembering that she had to get not only the viewers on side but also the other contestants, Chantelle began to indulge in the odd bit of flashing. Preston seemed rather impressed. 'Chantelle's boobs keep coming out, it's funny, innit?' he remarked to the Diary Room.

Breasts seemed to be on the agenda, with Jodie maintaining a spirited defence of her own décolletage. 'There are other celebrities,' she began, naming no names, 'who say, "That Jodie Marsh, she's got saggy tits," just because I don't pump them full of silicone.' She then turned her attention to Traci, saying, 'Big Brother probably doesn't have as good boobs as what Traci does.'

Rula and Pete decided to step in with some comforting advice for Jodie. Rula began by recommending the therapeutic effects of Buddhist chanting. '*I* chant,' said Pete.

'Really?' asked Rula, looking interested.

'Yeah. Fuck off, fuck off, fuck off, fuck off.'

The matter was closed.

It wasn't long, however, before high spirits, or, to put it more accurately, hard spirits, were making themselves felt again. Chantelle, Jodie and Traci all decided they needed to appreciate Dennis's charms more closely and began a bizarre form of four-in-a-bed romp with him, in which they fought to peel back the bedclothes to discover the full extent of his manliness. Dennis rather coyly fought back, managing to maintain his modesty, at which the trio trooped disconsolately back to the kitchen.

There, things turned ugly. Pete Burns, a transvestite cum plastic surgery aficionado, had a tongue as sharp as his appearance was outlandish, and began to take it out on the girls. First he condemned them for their behaviour, to which Traci responded by sitting on him and asking if he wanted some action. The answer was no. 'You have no idea how dirty I get, but here?' he replied. 'No way. Fuck right off.'

'She was just being friendly,' protested Jodie.

'Your tits are hanging out,' added Traci.

'Well, your dick is hanging out of your top as you're being a total dickhead,' was Mr Burns's reply.

Outside the house, someone who was watching all this with a very jaundiced eye was Dennis Rodman's first wife, Anicka Bakes. It was to become a feature of the series that, while the housemates partied on, happily unaware of what was going on outside, the public was being treated to a slightly different series of events, as people who had been associated with the housemates came forward to have their say. And Anicka's say was a scathing one. She and Rodman had previously been together for seven years, and had a daughter together, Alexis, who was now 17. Dennis went on to marry twice more, and at the time of the programme was still married to his third wife, Michelle Moyer, with whom he had two children, although they now lived apart. And, if what Anicka said about Dennis had any bearing on matters, Jodie, Traci and Chantelle would be very well advised to steer clear.

'You [Jodie, Traci and Chantelle] are stupid if you go anywhere near him' she said. Of course, the housemates were unaware of her warnings, but, as it turned out, none of the girls had anything to fear, as nothing developed between any of them and Dennis, but Anicka's remarks got a great deal of attention on the outside. *Big Brother* fever was by now at such a pitch that almost everything about the housemates was of consuming interest. It was that rarest of television programmes: something that the country wanted to discuss the morning after each show.

Past participants were all pretty fascinated by it as well. Kenzie, who just happened to be an ex-boyfriend of Jodie Marsh, as well as the runner-up in the 2005 *Celebrity Big Brother*, was dismissive of the current inmates. 'They're weird,' he said. 'Chantelle looks like one of the most genuine people. I think she'll do well and be a proper celebrity when she comes out. And I ain't one to judge, but it looks like Michael Barrymore is playing up to the cameras. I like Maggot. I think he could have it away.'

And what of Jodie? 'I was quite shocked when she went in, but I can see why she's done it,' said Kenzie. 'I think all she wants to do is prove to people what she's really like. She feels she's got a really bad stereotype around her, so she wants to set the record straight.'

Meanwhile, Tom Smith, of the Editors, was staggered that a fellow lead singer, albeit for another band, was taking part. Asked if he would do the same, he replied, 'No, definitely not. I can't think of anything worse. I'd rather stick pins in my eyes, to be honest.'

Back in the house, Jodie and Traci started cuddling, with Jodie announcing, 'I love Traci. She's gorgeous. If she kissed me, I'd kiss her.'

This was too much for Pete, who began snarling at Jodie and described her as 'a pumped-up, sucked-in little piece of crud', adding, 'Jodie has to stop crying; she can't cry for 21 days.'

Certainly, Jodie had been displaying a degree of weepiness. Clearly the worse for wear, she had been telling the housemates that she had been bullied since she was 11, and became so disconsolate that even Traci was heard to remark, 'Breakdown number two.' This might, of course, have been a clue to Jodie's excessive behaviour as an adult – at one point she disrobed fully in view of the *Big Brother* cameras – but the house was no place to start dealing with the traumas of the past. As the show progressed, there were serious concerns voiced on the outside as to the treatment Jodie received at the hands of the others, but the housemates, in their little cocoon, were oblivious to the outside world.

And Jodie was not helping herself. 'It's tough being me,' she said earlier in the evening, already in tears. 'I've been bullied. I've been told I was ugly every day since I was 11 years old.'

Dennis initially attempted to sympathise, but then headed outdoors for a cigar, muttering, 'I just don't give a shit.'

As for Pete, his viciousness intensified throughout that evening. 'At the end of the day, if you get your tits out, people are going to have an opinion,' he said. 'Go on, Jodie. Have another drink and let it come flooding out of your tear ducts. Anyone who cries should be publicly flogged.'

It might have made for horribly compulsive viewing, but it was undeniably a study in cruelty and, self-obsessed and unhappy as Jodie appeared to be, she came out immeasurably better than Pete did. After all this, the interplay between George and Rula came as a relief.

Already the ultimate make-up of the household was beginning to reveal itself. There were to be shifts of allegiances over the coming weeks: early friendships turned sour, rivalries emerged and tempers quite often frayed, but some patterns that were to remain were already obvious. Pete never let up once during his entire time in the house: nothing and no one was exempt from his observations, although he was clearly harsher on the women than he was on the men.

Jodie, alas, was weepy pretty much throughout her time in the house and didn't really make lasting friends during her stay. Dennis was and remained interested in women. Barrymore was a more complex case: viewers saw someone who was clearly a deeply troubled man: his constant restlessness during the night and inability to relax hinted at the inner conflicts that had led to his difficult behaviour in the past. George and Rula were to change during their time in the household: both as far as the viewers saw them and in relation to each other.

Chantelle, however, had started as she meant to go on: bright and breezy. She certainly didn't appear to have an action plan and, indeed, her initial ploy was simply to make sure she stayed in the house. No one, as yet, had a clue about how everything would turn out.

All in all, it was a mixed and unpredictable group that awaited the first of the *Big Brother* challenges. Now that the housemates had settled in, it was time for them to sing for their supper – quite literally, in the case of Chantelle. The house was mounting a 'show and tell' showcase, in which the various celebs were set tasks: those who failed were to have only £1 each per day to spend on food. Chantelle's challenge was to sing 'I Want It Right Now', the hit she had supposedly had with Kandyfloss, and she was to be given just one chance to practise it before performing in front of her housemates.

It was a nerve-racking time: she was up in front of real singers and massively experienced entertainers. A member of a real girl band could be forgiven for having nerves; someone whose showbiz experience was confined to modelling and work as a lookalike could be forgiven for being paralysed with fear. But Chantelle wasn't. The producers had clearly done their homework before putting her in the show, for, if she had bottled it at the outset, her appearance would have been meaningless. Putting her in the house would only work if she was able to participate as a full member of the household – and that she did.

Whoever set the challenges must have had a sense of humour. Faria Alam was to deliver a 90-second speech on 'Why I Am Famous', as was Jodie. Traci had to give a demonstration of running in slow motion in a swimming costume. Maggot and Pete were also told to sing. Dennis had to perform a slam dunk and spin a baseball on his finger. Barrymore had to write and perform a 90-second sketch on a topic he could choose. Rula had to perform a monologue from *Macbeth*.

But all eyes were on Chantelle, at least from outside the house, where the viewers were in on the secret. And in the event, as the world now knows, she pulled it off. She was no Barbra Streisand when it came to her voice, but then, in girl bands these days, who is? Despite being off-key and forgetting some of the words, somehow she got away with it, for all the embarrassed looks from the others and

Dennis's snorts of laughter. 'Very good, Chantelle,' said George kindly. 'I'll buy it.'

It was by no means a bravura performance, but such was the buzz now surrounding her that there was speculation that she might later release a single. 'Chantelle's dodgy voice may not prevent her from hitting the charts when she gets out of the house,' said David Williams of Ladbrokes, offering odds of 25/1 that she would do just that. 'Punters have taken her to their hearts, and are keen to live the dream with her.' More surprisingly still, there was even talk of her fronting a UK version of Paris Hilton's show *The Simple Life*. The odds? Only 33/1.

The possibilities of what might happen next as part of Chantelle's transformation into a celebrity were only now coming to light. It's not clear if the producers knew what they were unleashing when they took an unknown and placed her in a household full of the famous and the nearly famous. Perhaps they were simply as interested as anyone else to see what the outcome would be. But no one had expected that the show would turn Chantelle into what she wanted to be and it's not stretching it to say that she is probably now better known than some of the other inhabitants of the house. This was the kind of televisual experiment that had never been tried before and, it must be said, it needed someone like Chantelle to carry it off.

It's also not clear whether Chantelle herself realised what would happen to her after she'd been on the show. Yes, she wanted to be famous, but surviving the *Celebrity Big Brother* household was more of a challenge than anything else. She still had to maintain a false identity in front of the others, which meant that, although she could show personality traits that were genuinely her own, she couldn't show the other contestants or the viewers the person she really was. What is clear is that she realised from the start that this was an opportunity, although she didn't realise just how big it was. But she knew that, if she pulled this off, greater things would follow.

As so often happens when a person finds celebrity for the first time, especially in a show like this, people from Chantelle's past began to emerge, in this case in the form of an ex-boyfriend. Keith Webster, a labourer from Wickford, had originally met Chantelle in a Basildon nightclub and fell for her immediately. He was now keen to tell his story: after all, now that his former girlfriend was in the process of becoming a genuine celebrity, the glamour somehow rubbed off.

'She looked great with her blonde hair and was wearing a short tight skirt which showed off her legs,' Keith said. 'We started chatting and got on straight away. I was used to everyone looking at her all the time we went out. It's just something you have to accept when you go out with a good-looking girl like her. Everyone loved her and she was even up for going out with the lads. Normally, it is embarrassing taking a girl out with the boys but with her it was cool.'

Alas, Chantelle was more concerned about her career than settling down. 'I wanted the relationship to go further but she was doing well with her modelling and wanted to get into it more, so she chose her career over me,' said a philosophical Keith. 'I felt a bit rough after we split but you get over these things. But she was always talking about being famous and I knew that is what she really wanted more than anything else.'

And, as so many people were to comment, this hunger for fame for its own sake, without necessarily having done a great deal to achieve it, is a particularly modern phenomenon. It fed on itself, making it entirely understandable that so many people would see it as a gateway to a better life. Members of the public like Jade Goody had been transported not just from anonymity to celebrity, but from modest circumstances to wealth. The downside, of course, is that the fame can be ephemeral and, once gone, is forever missed. But that did not stop the hordes who looked to *Big Brother* and other reality shows from trying their best. They knew that, if their gamble worked, it could completely change their lives.

Certainly, Chantelle's friends and family had always known that she wanted to be famous. 'I didn't even know about her being on *Celebrity Big Brother* until I saw it on TV and I saw this blonde who I recognised,' said Keith. 'It took me a while, then it dawned on me that it was Chantelle. I wondered when she had become a celebrity. At first I thought she had made it but then I realised she was just a faker. Of course, she will be famous after this now.' He couldn't have spoken a truer word. Chantelle was well on her way to becoming famous by this time – not that she had any idea yet of what was happening on the outside.

And it seemed no one had a bad word to say about her. In the world of wannabe stardom, it is only too easy to make enemies, but Chantelle seemed genuinely to be held in many people's affections, including that of her ex. 'Chantelle is your typical girl next door,' Keith said. 'Everyone knows her and likes her. She is popular with everyone and friendly back. I have never known her to have any enemies. She is a really sweet girl who takes a lot of pride over her appearance.

'Sometimes she would keep me waiting when we were going out by taking ages to get ready, but all girls do that. She is just a regular Essex girl. She hasn't got expensive tastes. She would be just as happy with a night at the local pub as she would in a flash bar or restaurant. Chantelle is a very truthful and honest girl. She is lovely and lots of fun. She has always wanted to be famous and now she has got what she wants. I wish her well.'

But Chantelle was by no means the only figure of fascination for the public: the others were also doing a great deal to keep the outside world agog. Secrets were coming out thick and fast, with Jodie revealing that she once took revenge on an ex with dubious personal-hygiene habits by leaving a bag of washing outside so that everyone could see how filthy he was. Faria went one better. 'Have you ever pissed in someone's tea?' she asked. 'I did – of a boyfriend who I didn't like.'

'Did you watch him drink it?' Chantelle was curious to know.

'Yeah, that was the best part,' said Faria.

Of course, immediately afterwards there was a great deal of speculation as to who the unlucky guy was. Faria has still not revealed his name.

But it was Jodie who was drawing most attention to herself and, sadly, she was doing herself no favours. The poor girl was coming in for some serious flak from Pete by now. In fact, so vicious was he becoming that it was quite reminiscent of the tension between Jodie's nemesis Jordan and John Lydon, aka Johnny Rotten, on *I'm A Celebrity... Get Me Out Of Here!*, in which Johnny constantly had a go at Jordan and Jordan constantly fought back. But Jordan was clearly made of much sterner stuff than Jodie, who really was allowing it to get to her – and no wonder, given the vitriol flying her way.

Rula, at least, tried to calm everyone down, returning to the subject of chanting. 'We all have a Buddhist god within us, we just have to tap into it,' she explained, although the viewer couldn't help but wonder where her own Buddhist god had been in the middle of her fraught marriage to Dennis Waterman. 'If you chant positive things, the universe has a way of paying you back in a positive way.'

But Pete was not chanting positive thoughts. He was chanting his views about Jodie to Barrymore. 'She goes on about people saying she's got saggy tits and that she's fat,' he hissed, adding, in a reference to one of Jodie's more extravagant outfits, 'If that's the case, would you go up there, wearing two belts, when they hang out all over the place?

'With cut-off jeans that are too small, pissed and slurring your words? She says she needs intellectual stimulation like food but I think she's either thick as pig shit, needs help or it's calculated to inflict guilt.

"'Oh, my dog died. I burned the toast. People say my boobs are saggy.'"

Barrymore was a little gentler. 'I couldn't say I don't like her, but I'm cringing,' he said. 'If she doesn't want to be perceived as the whore of Babylon, she'd better start thinking.'

Pete, who was fast becoming the most controversial figure on the show, had perhaps taken his row with Jodie too far: in a further ill-tempered exchange, he claimed to be wearing a gorilla-skin coat. This upset not just the model, but also the Department for Environment, Food and Rural Affairs.

'Gorilla skins belong on gorillas, not on reality-TV show contestants,' said Minister for Biodiversity Jim Knight, who warned Pete that he could spend up to five years in prison for trading in an endangered species. 'Gorillas are critically endangered, and any promotion of gorilla products in this country can only put these amazing creatures in further peril. If this is, in fact, a gorilla skin, there may be serious consequences. Any gorilla skin acquired after June 1947 would require an exemption permit, which would be highly unlikely to be granted. Equally, any gorilla skins or other products brought into this country require an import permit.'

The row was to continue for some time. In an animal-loving country like Britain, Pete's claim was bound to provoke an outcry and it did. There was intensive speculation as to whether the coat was really a gorilla skin and intensive condemnation for Pete for wearing it, whatever it turned out to be. Of course, he didn't know of the commotion his comments provoked, but he would have been delighted. He was a professional controversialist: what some of the others in the house didn't perhaps realise was that he was there to cause mayhem. The producers had chosen the mix of housemates very carefully: they were well aware that Pete was likely to cause outrage and upset.

Nor was Pete alone in raising eyebrows in the outside world. There were increasing concerns at the presence of George among the group, not least because it meant that he was neglecting his work as an MP. A key event in the political life of the country was coming up: a debate on the £500-million Crossrail transport link, which would affect his constituency of Bethnal Green and Bow, and his constituents were decidedly unamused that he wasn't going to be there to have his say. In fact, so annoyed were they that they had started a protest campaign on the internet entitled 'Get Back To Work George' and had calculated how much it cost taxpayers for each day that their MP stayed away. To date it was £643.

But Galloway was unaware of the furore gathering momentum outside. His concerns were domestic: indeed, it was he who broke the news of the next crisis to hit the household: the loo paper had run out. After a visit to the bathroom, he marched grimly through the household muttering, 'I'm looking for toilet paper.'

The housemates took this as seriously as they should. 'This is true humiliation,' growled Rula. 'In Poland before communism fell, if you were in a nightclub you had to ask for two sheets of paper and had to pay for them. And if you wanted to do something more than a wee, you had to go through the humiliation of saying two sheets is not enough.'

'I suppose I could cut up some carpet tiles and use those,' suggested Barrymore.

Faria, who was now deemed something of an expert on the subject, rose to the occasion. 'Flushing carpet down the toilet isn't a good idea,' she said.

Amid such drama, triumph was approaching for Chantelle. The next task set for the housemates was to line up in order of their fame, deciding among themselves how famous they all were. There were 11 in the house and, if Chantelle came in at number 11, that was it – she was out. In the event, she actually made it to the ninth spot, with Preston one place behind her and the title of least famous housemate going to Maggot. Chantelle herself didn't immediately realise the scale of her victory, and when summoned to the Diary Room she was convinced she was going to be evicted. 'What's going on?' she asked. Meanwhile, *Big Brother* anointed her an official celebrity, much to the bemusement of the other housemates, who were watching the proceedings on a big screen, before more alcohol was brought into the house and a party was had by all.

There was one person who was pretty irate about the whole process: George Galloway. The final line-up had him at number four, after Pete, Dennis and Barrymore: 'If it's worldwide, then I should be number one,' he snapped. 'Virtually every Muslim in the world knows who I am.'

And Pete took yet another opportunity to have a go at his favourite victim. 'Jodie's a complete imbecile,' he said. 'She's harming herself on a public platform. She's got the mental capacity of a nine-year-old. You can take the whore to culture, but you can't make her think.'

Nor was George Galloway particularly impressed by Jodie's behaviour. It was clear that he could hardly bear the overt way she was conducting herself. On one occasion in the Diary Room, he talked about her 'extraordinary stories at the breakfast table, which involve every orifice and every fluid known to man'. He hoped his daughter would never speak like that, he said, before asking, 'Does that make me old-fashioned?' But Jodie wasn't the only person who offended him. 'Every comment Dennis makes is about the size of his organ,' he complained. 'What's all that about?'

But he did have a point. On another occasion, Jodie remarked to him, 'I've had orgies before. Five of us. Best night of my life. Up for an orgy, George?' George ignored her and puffed irritably on his cigar. Her charms were making no impression here.

Rula agreed with George, proclaiming herself 'shocked at the amount of sexual innuendo', while he said heroically, 'When you see people coming on to each other in a grotesque way, I have a duty to step in. The public who know me would expect it.'

3

Mad About the Girl

Out in the real world, Chantelle was being increasingly talked about. Growing numbers of viewers were becoming susceptible to her charm: she was no Einstein, but her rather off-the-wall comments were gaining a following. One that was picked up was when she asked George Galloway if he worked in the house with all the green seats. Then there was her admission that she didn't know what a gynaecologist was. It was all grist to the mill.

The public liked the fact that she was already behaving like a star, too. 'We managed to get her three bookings and she only turned up to one,' said her agent, as more details about her past life began to emerge. It seemed a splendidly insouciant way to behave and it went down well with viewers. In fact, the only time she raised eyebrows was when she swore on her mother's life that she was a celebrity, something she later said she regretted. She was winning hearts and minds outside the house just as much as she was within.

It was not just Chantelle whose life was being changed by the shenanigans going on in the house. She was, of course, now a bona fide celebrity, but the others, despite the fact that they were already real celebrities to varying degrees, were also doing well out of it. Preston's band the Ordinary Boys had been almost as little known as Chantelle herself before he entered the house, but, as a result of the exposure he was getting, their album *Brassbound* was selling better than it ever had done before. The same was happening to the band Goldie Lookin Chain, which boasted Maggot among its members. As for Pete Burns – the one-time lead singer of Dead Or Alive had kick-started sales of *The Best of Dead Or Alive*, trebling the number of copies shifted.

And, as the celebrities themselves knew, appearing in a show like this could kick-start a career. Ever since Tony Blackburn had come first in *I'm A Celebrity… Get Me Out Of Here!* some years earlier, everyone whose star had been fading, who had been out of the public eye for some time or who needed a boost to their profile knew quite how helpful a show like this could be. Of the current lot, of course, no one was more aware of this than Michael Barrymore, who was using the show as a way of testing his popularity with the British public. But it was having an effect on the rest of the inmates of the house, too.

This was recognised on the outside. 'We sometimes wonder why any celebrity would put themselves through *Big Brother*, but now I think we have the answer,' said Gideon Lask of HMV. 'These guys have only been in the house for a few days and, while admittedly building from a rather low sales base at this time of year, they are already seeing some benefit to their recording careers. Who knows, perhaps Chantelle may have a career with Kandyfloss after all. Reality TV seems to make anything possible these days.'

It certainly did, but then so much depended on the luck of the draw and what the housemates had to contend with next was that most feared moment in reality television: eviction. Here was another potentially catastrophic moment for Chantelle. Her housemates had been let into the secret and there was every possibility that they would seek revenge by nominating her. But in the end she survived.

For it was three quite different people who were chosen for eviction first: Jodie Marsh, who received eight nominations, and George Galloway and Pete Burns, who got four each. Poor Jodie was certainly not popular: the only two not to have voted for her were Chantelle and Preston, whereas all the others were clear about why she was their nominee.

'She's a very troublesome element and a very troublesome person,' said George Galloway. 'She neither cooks nor cleans; she's sexually obsessed of the crudest variety.' But then nor was he particularly enamoured of Pete, calling him 'the housemate from hell'.

It was almost inevitable that Pete would nominate Jodie. 'I don't like occupying the same space as her,' he said in a typically full-on diatribe. 'Some of her views on things I find absolutely abhorrent to my principles.'

Michael Barrymore, hardly an example of a straightforward personality himself, also nominated Jodie because she had not taken his advice on how to live her life. 'I'm trying to help mend other people,' he explained.

Poor old Jodie herself took it pretty well, all things considered. 'I honestly think all things happen for a reason,' she said sadly. 'If I'm first out, then so be it. If I'm not first out, then being nominated first will make me stronger. All I wanted to get out of it was for people to see me.'

If truth be told, even if she didn't see it that way at the time, it was probably best for everyone if Jodie were to go. She was utterly miserable in the house and appeared to become more so by the day. While the show can have miraculous effects on some people's careers, it doesn't work for everyone, and Jodie had certainly not been a beneficiary of its magic. She was also bringing down the other housemates, who veered between irritation and unkindness. Chantelle was the only one who seemed to have warmed to Jodie at all.

The other two housemates took it rather better. Galloway, on hearing the news, merely shrugged and said, 'I'm going back to bed,' whereas Pete didn't even comment. Given the virulence of his comments, it is almost inconceivable that he didn't realise there was a very real chance that he might be the first to go. In the event, though, he wasn't, for the simple reason that his entertainment value outweighed his difficult side.

But it is hard not to suspect that Galloway was put out. In a profession crammed full of overbearing egos, his is still capable of standing out and, of course, he had no idea how he was coming across on the outside. As far as he was concerned, he was making politics more accessible to a younger generation and doubtless he thought that he was entertaining the nation while so doing. He was right there – although perhaps not in quite the way he assumed.

Ironically, it would almost certainly have been far better for him if he had got out at this stage. Like Jodie, Galloway was not to benefit from his time in the house – quite the opposite, in fact – and, had he left nearer the start, he would have been spared some of the more excruciating moments still to come. But one of the many reasons that *Big Brother* works so well is that the people who elect to appear on it are so often completely lacking in self-knowledge, as well as not understanding that the show's producers will angle everything to suit them. So Galloway was to stay on and the world was to watch as he dug himself even deeper into a hole.

Naturally, the bookies were on the case, ranking Jodie as the clear favourite to leave first. Her odds were 1/3, with Galloway following at 2/1 and Pete Burns bringing up the rear with 8/1. 'The writing is on the wall,' said a solemn David Williams from Ladbrokes. Galloway wasn't doing too well himself, if it came to that: there had already been a great deal of speculation about how the mainly Muslim vote that got him into parliament would be taking his antics on the show. There were already odds of 2/5 that he would lose his seat at the next general election. 'This adventure has done George Galloway no good at all and it will definitely count against him when he is up for election,' said Paul Petrie of Totesport. Within the *Big Brother* house itself, the sands were also shifting: until now, the favourite to win the show had been Michael Barrymore. But Preston had now inched forward to become the 2/1 favourite to win.

As for Chantelle, she was going from strength to strength. She was loving every minute of it, especially now that she was officially a celebrity herself. But fame would not change her, she said. 'If a tramp on the street comes up to me, I'll chat with him.' Actually, by the time she finally got out, a tramp would have had no chance whatsoever of getting close to her: as a real celeb, she was quite beyond the touch of the hoi polloi. But now she was really happy – and there was still over two weeks to go.

As the cameras rolled in the house, so interest in Chantelle continued to mount even more intensively in the outside world. All the popular papers were working hard at digging up as much as they could about her and her past, and trying to shed light on this most mysterious of phenomena: the celebrity who became a celebrity by pretending to be a celebrity. And she didn't even know herself how famous she'd become – yet.

It was known by now that Chantelle came from Wickford in Essex and that she'd spent some time as a barmaid in the Duke, but the locals proved very loyal to her. 'Alan [Chantelle's father] still drinks here most days and he has decided he's not talking about his daughter,' said one. 'For that reason, you'll find most people in here won't have anything to say because it just wouldn't be fair. All I will say is that I knew her before she went on the show and what you see on TV is what you get in real life. She's a typical Essex blonde – down-to-earth, cheeky and fun. I think achieving fame has always been a real motivation for her. Now she's got it, I just hope she knows what to do with it.'

Other than that, it emerged that Chantelle lived with her mother, Vivien, 47, a legal secretary, and Vivien's partner, Dean, 36, who ran a removal firm in Brentwood, in a £200,000 three-bedroom detached house on a 1960s estate. And, apart from the revelations by an ex-boyfriend, that was it. During her time in the house, a great deal more was to come out about Chantelle, but for now, at least, her origins lay shrouded in mystery. That suited the producers down to the ground, as they wanted to encourage as much speculation and excitement about their new star as they could.

And it was working. 'The whole thing is very clever,' said Max Clifford, the PR guru who probably knows more than anyone else in the country about turning nobodies into celebs. 'The obvious point is that anyone these days can be famous. You don't need talent, you don't need ability. So much of it is to do with absolutely nothing. It's not too difficult for Chantelle to be convincing because she looks like everyone's idea of a footballer's wife or a kiss-and-tell girl. The other contestants don't know of each other because most of them are non-entities, so Chantelle fits in perfectly. It shows how absurd the whole thing is, which is why it works for people watching at home. The irony is that she is going to become famous for pretending to be famous.'

But how long would it last? The history of reality TV is littered with people who became famous for a short time and then, within months or even weeks, found themselves back in obscurity, yearning for a fame that only so fleetingly was theirs. Would the same thing happen to Chantelle? 'She could earn more money in the next year than she has in the last six or seven years,' said Clifford. 'She could make £100,000, maybe more. [But] her shelf life will be five minutes. Other than getting another reality programme, I imagine she'll disappear as quickly as the others. What I suggest she does is make a few bob while she can and after that she can always work as a lookalike for herself.'

At the time of writing, that is not what has happened. Chantelle is now not only more famous than she was when she was inside the house, but her fame is still growing. And she has made far more than £100,000. There seems to be every chance that she'll be able to build a real career on her time in the *Big Brother* house, with all the opportunities and rivalries that entails. This did not please everyone, particularly the established celebrities on whose turf she was trampling. Even the glamour model Jordan has reportedly become displeased about this woman she sees as a rival, not least because Chantelle is now, too, part of a famous couple. In fact, signs of that future pairing were already emerging within the house.

By now, Chantelle and Jodie had pressed their charms upon Dennis and, fuelled by a certain amount of alcohol, decided that Preston would be their next victim. 'If I could shag anyone in here, just for a laugh, it would be Preston,' said the ever-game Jodie.

'He's fit,' agreed Chantelle.

They kicked off their mission by creeping to the Diary Room and announcing plans to snog Preston, before Chantelle went into the bedroom and managed to get their target – who, incidentally, had a girlfriend called Camille – to come and join her for a chat. Once they were there, Maggot and Pete joined, followed shortly by Jodie, who pushed her chest into Maggot's face. 'I can't breathe!' he cried.

'They're like airbags,' observed Pete.

With that, the boys all fled, so Chantelle and Jodie sidled off and hid in Preston's bed. The lucky man himself appeared shortly afterwards. 'We're ready for you!' called the girls, an invitation Preston seemed disinclined to turn down: he leaped on to the bed and started hugging both of them. Big Brother, however, appeared unmoved by this show of youthful exuberance, and summoned Preston to the Diary Room, a lull in the proceedings that the girls took advantage of by striking a series of poses. 'It's better than blonde on blonde,' remarked Chantelle. 'It's blonde on dark.' They then climbed back into Preston's bed, only to be turfed out of it when the man himself returned. 'I'm offended, but there it is,' Jodie remarked.

That was the first time anyone had a hint of what was to come. From very early on, there was an attraction between Preston and Chantelle, one that became increasingly obvious to viewers and, alas, to Camille as the series progressed. To be fair to the parties concerned, it was a very difficult situation. Preston had a girlfriend outside to whom he owed loyalty, but he found himself increasingly drawn to someone else and, to cap it all, his feelings were being broadcast live to the nation. He did everything he could to disguise those feelings, but it was obvious what was beginning to happen.

The same applied, to a lesser extent, to Chantelle. Various insinuations have been made about whether she had anyone waiting for her when she came out of the house, but what was undoubtedly true was that she was not in a serious relationship the way Preston was. However, she had her own issues. This was her big chance: the opportunity to become famous in her own right. But, at exactly the time she was giving it her all, she also had become aware of an attraction to one of her housemates that might well have put her off her stride. In the end, it didn't – in fact, popular opinion was that the relationship between the two was charming – but it was a difficult situation for everyone to deal with.

That was not the only bit of salaciousness on the show that week. Someone had put extra-large condoms on the house's shopping list, but the identity of that person was kept a secret, although it was said that it couldn't be Dennis as he'd already brought a stash of the things into the house. Then

Preston decided to admit to wearing girl's jeans – 'I like them nice and tight' – while Traci and Dennis announced to Chantelle that they spied on her when she was getting dressed. When Chantelle became upset at the news, Dennis reacted strongly. 'You're being filmed,' he said. 'The whole world has been watching you.'

Despite his earlier coyness, Dennis now seemed keen to live up to his reputation as a lady's man. After some heavy-duty flirting with both Chantelle and Jodie, he turned his attentions to Faria, who seemed remarkably unimpressed by her new suitor. First, he put his hand under her top and a slightly tight-lipped Faria removed it. A discussion about sugar-daddies ensued. 'I hope some 97-year-old, blind, paraplegic billionaire sugar-daddy is watching this, so I can leave him outside Tiffany's while I use his credit card before wheeling him home,' mused Pete. 'And me and my partner could go and live with him and he wouldn't even know.'

Dennis, rather brilliantly, leaped into action. 'Do you love me?' he enquired of Faria.

'What did you ask me? Do I love you? Of course I do, darling,' Faria replied.

'Can I be your sugar-daddy?' Dennis continued.

'You're only three years older than me,' said Faria patiently.

'OK, you can be my sugar-mamma,' suggested Dennis.

'I'm younger than you, Dennis,' said Faria. 'So that's not a good idea.'

'Can I be useful in other ways?' asked Dennis.

'No,' Faria replied.

The housemates' allotted tasks remained as daft as ever. Pete and Dennis were each given pot plants to nurture and to test the theory that talking to them helps them to grow. 'I hate plants,' said Pete. 'I hope it dies.'

Barrymore, meanwhile, was given the task of smashing eggs against his forehead in order to answer the question 'Can you make yourself unlucky?', while Preston was ordered to eat his way through innumerable boxes of chocolate liqueurs to see if they made him drunk. Happily, all the housemates survived their various ordeals.

While all of this was going on, rather more serious issues were also coming to light. Jodie was not presenting herself in the best way possible in *Celebrity Big Brother* or, for that matter, in her outside life, and she was clearly becoming increasingly distressed about the way she was being treated within the house. After yet another row, this one with Barrymore and Pete, she burst out, 'I might as well kill myself, because I have nothing to live for.'

The row had been even uglier than those which had erupted before. Barrymore called her 'a liar', adding, 'You talk such a load of shit.'

'At least I don't leave the country when I face difficulties,' Jodie spat back.

In Barrymore's eyes, this was pressing the nuclear button, referring as it did to the fact that he had gone to live in New Zealand after his career had imploded in the UK. There had been a great deal of speculation on whether and when this would come up. The whole country had been waiting to see if Barrymore would talk about his recent ordeals and indeed whether he would talk about his new life generally. The comic was, despite everything, an unknown commodity in many ways. Obviously a tortured personality, he was neither a villain nor a saint. No one could predict with certainty how he would cope in the house and no one really knew how he felt about everything that had happened in recent years. But, at that point, at least, no one was going to find out.

'We try to help you,' he told Jodie, having just insulted her, 'but you don't listen. What planet are you on?'

She took this even more to heart and started to talk about the fact that her father had not been able to see her into the house because he was ill, on top of which she had been booed on entering the place.

'I find it painful that you sacrifice yourself at the altar of public opinion,' said Pete, clearly in no mood to mend bridges, before informing Jodie that her arch-rival Jordan was clearly a bright woman.

As it happened, every celebrity in the house was supporting a charity, and Jodie's was Beatbullying, for which she was also an ambassador after having survived years of bullying at school. The organisation was so concerned at what it saw as the harsh treatment of her that it spoke out at this point. 'Beatbullying has received a huge number of emails from young people across the UK who support Jodie's stance on bullying, many of them very worried about some of the treatment Jodie is going through in the *Big Brother* house,' said a spokesman.

'Beatbullying will speak out against bullying whenever it happens. We will continue to support Jodie through her journey. Like all of the young people we work with, we know Jodie is strong and will stand up against bullies whenever she meets them.'

The charity was not alone. Quite a few commentators had voiced concerns about Jodie's situation: she might not have put herself in a good

hantelle performs her song 'I want it right now' for the right to stay in the *Celebrity
g Brothe*r house: she succeeds, and a star is born.

Above: Kissing Preston on the cheek while *Baywatch* star Traci Bingham is the gooseberry in the *Celebrity Big Brother* diary room.

Below: Getting cosy with Preston – a romance was soon underway.

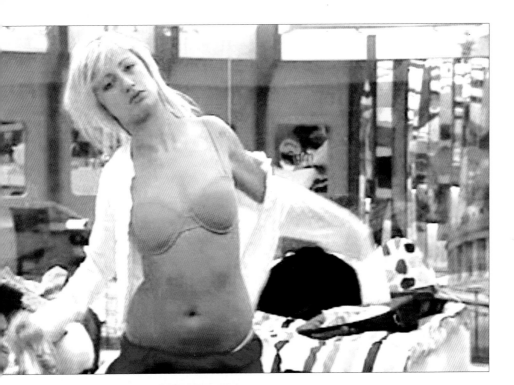

above: Rise and shine Chantelle!

below: Ask a stupid question! With Maggot in the diary room.

Above: With Jodie Marsh, who had a tough time in the house.

Below: Chantelle gets another chance to perform – this time doing Riverdance with Michael Barrymore.

bove: Jodie, Preston and Chantelle enjoy a relaxing moment.

elow: 'Oh my God!' Chantelle hears the news that will change her life forever – she has

ɔn *Celebrity Big Brother*!

Chantelle leaves the house a bona fide celebrity.

om delight, to shock and then laughter… Chantelle relives her time in the house with *lebrity Big Brother* presenter Davina McCall.

Reunited at last: Chantelle embraces Preston after leaving the house, while the nation wonders what the future holds for the couple.

light but surely, the thinking went, she deserved better treatment from the others than this.

Her parents, too, were watching what was happening to their daughter with increasing concern. 'I think she will liken the house to her schooldays,' said Kristina Marsh. 'This is exactly what happened then. There was one strong person at school – exactly like George Galloway – that turned everyone against her. I don't know how much longer she will be able to cope with that.'

Jodie's mother continued that, while she and her husband had been happy for her to take part in a reality-television show, none of them could have foreseen what Jodie was letting herself in for. 'We had no idea just how bad it would be and we don't think she had any idea what she was going into. She has seen it before, but I don't think she realised how much people would be going up against her… basically, she's been ostracised.'

John Marsh, Jodie's father, was equally concerned, opining that Michael Barrymore had serious problems of his own that he was taking out on Jodie. 'He's screaming at her to shut her mouth and telling her not to criticise anyone, when he is criticising her,' he said. 'This is Jodie's job. She was looking forward to going in; we didn't mind at all. We knew she was going to be in with a lot of competition, that's what it's all about, but we didn't expect her to be bullied by three middle-aged men… one of which is a third-rate politician who claims to be a gentleman when he isn't.'

Jodie's friend Sarah Blight was also worried about her. 'She is in there on her own with no allies fighting against the most cruel and calculating bullies,' she said. 'They simply should know better at their age and I am sure they would be outraged if someone ganged up on a child of theirs in the same way. I think it is particularly sad that they do not stop until they make her cry either and then attempt to insinuate that her tears aren't real.'

For by now Jodie was being ostracised by everyone except kind-hearted Chantelle, who, Galloway announced, had been put under a wicked spell by Jodie. But now even Pete was beginning to express some doubts over whether they had all behaved in the best way. 'It may be being really cruel to her,' he said to Barrymore, 'but, if we all turned hostile on her now, she could walk out and say, "I was driven from the *Big Brother* house by 50-year-olds." Everyone would feel sorry for her… sobbing on the top of the steps as she fled the building in two belts.'

In truth, a feeling of unease about the treatment of Jodie was beginning to spread throughout the house.

Maggot seemed torn, one minute saying that he 'didn't like negative energy' and the next saying it was her own fault. Barrymore also said he felt sorry for her. There was a sense that matters had got out of hand, that what might have started as rather harsh teasing had turned too nasty. No one was entirely comfortable with what had been going on.

And this is one of the side issues of the very premise of the show: locking a number of complete strangers in a house together is bound to throw up some tensions that are too strong to handle. Cut off from reality, the group found it all too easy to forget what constituted normal behaviour, and this was what was happening now. The truth of the matter is that, although Jodie was being self-indulgent and melodramatic, the men were being far too harsh on her. But the same kind of behaviour surfaced again after she had left. With none of the normal constraints and nothing to temper aggression, some of the housemates – particularly George Galloway – were prone to overreact. Even so, they should have realised that they were going too far.

Poor old Jodie was so overwrought that she might well have walked out at this point, but for the fact that she, like the others, had a contract that specified that if she did so she wouldn't get paid. On course to earn £30,000 for her stay, she herself put it this way:

'If I didn't need the money, I would have walked by now. I just don't want to be here any more.'

This possibility was one that the programme makers were well aware of. 'We were worried a few of the celebs could turn up for a couple of days and then decide to quit, knowing they would keep most of their fee,' said an insider on the show. 'So we devised tighter contracts than normal that had a bigger emphasis on staying in until you're voted out. Normally, if someone is in there for a week and then quits, they still pick up a decent pay day, but not this time.'

It emerged that the other two they had been particularly worried about had been Pete Burns, who was said to be getting £50,000 for his presence in the house but who usually had other people to pander to his every whim, and Michael Barrymore, who, on £150,000, was getting the biggest whack but who had shown himself to be less than stable in the past. Of the others, Galloway was earning £60,000; Rula £35,000; Dennis £90,000; Traci £75,000; Faria £35,000; Maggot £20,000 and Preston £25,000. Chantelle's fee was unknown, but the potential financial upside, should she make a name for herself in the house, was so great that its size didn't really matter. The kind of exposure that she was getting was beyond what money could buy.

Chantelle also had something on her mind. Earlier, she had sworn on her mother's life that she was a real celebrity, but now she was having a real fit of remorse. 'I'm really happy to be in here,' she said rather tearfully in the Diary Room. 'And really happy that I passed my mission. But I feel awful that I swore that in the pool to Preston. In the back of my head I was going, "Not really, not really, not really." I feel really horrible about it and guilty.'

Her fellow celebs were understanding. 'Your mum will understand,' said Faria.

'Your mum knows how much you love her and she's going to be so proud of you,' Jodie told her. 'She's going to be rooting for you now.'

It is telling, incidentally, that, for all the fact that Chantelle was the only 'fake' celebrity in the house, these two other women certainly had no more claim to fame than she did – if anything, less. Jodie had founded an entire career on having oversized breasts and taking her top off, while Faria had become known for the number of affairs she had had at the Football Association. Chantelle, on the other hand, was actually trying to do something to make herself famous. It took guts to go into the house as she had done, and to hold her own in that company was not always easy. But she was managing and becoming more accomplished with every day that passed.

Outside, others were becoming impressed, too. A budget hotel chain was considering offering her a £100,000-a-year advertising deal. 'Travelodge rooms cost from a tenner a night,' said spokesman Greg Dawson. 'That's a down-to-earth price that Chantelle's image would communicate brilliantly.' Meanwhile, her mother had signed her up with Max Clifford, prompting ever more speculation about what her future held when she emerged from the house. As it happened, Travelodge was not going to remain on the agenda, but an awful lot more was. Chantelle's appearance on the show was to be a big hit. But even at this stage no one realised just how spectacular that success would be.

4

Jim'll Fix It

It was at this point that a truly memorable *Big Brother* moment occurred. Every series had one: a scene that stayed in viewers' minds and was repeated over and over on television itself, to the great discomfort of the participants. And this one was not only embarrassing for the people involved, although they were not to know how it had been portrayed until they left the house, but provoked real anger in some quarters. It was, of course, the scene in which George Galloway, MP, founding member of the Respect Party and self-proclaimed champion of the underdog, pretended to be a cat.

It all began when Big Brother set the contestants a

task to see whether they could read the minds of animals. Galloway pretended to be a lab assistant, while Rula 'read the mind' of a goldfish called Barry, after which, in a moment he must have later regretted, Galloway asked Rula if she would like him to be a cat. When she agreed, the member for Bethnal Green and Bow got on all fours and crawled around her, while pretending to lick cream from her hands. Clearly, he had no idea whatsoever how he was coming across as he mewled and cooed and rubbed his head against Rula. This image was later to be reprinted on the front of *Private Eye*, with a speech balloon coming out of Galloway's mouth saying, 'And then Saddam said, "You can get up now."'

Either the two must have forgotten that the cameras were taking all this in or, at the very least, thought viewers would see it as mere high spirits and jollity. The scene grew ever more cringe-worthy as Rula rubbed the cream from his whiskers, stroked his head and behind his ears, the two of them throughout maintaining a dialogue so saccharine and yet so ghastly in its coyness that it will haunt the two of them for many a year to come. The overall impression was of some dreadful sexual role-play, quite as awful as any suggestion Jodie had come up with. It made most of the front pages the next day and provoked absolute fury from George's east London constituency and parliament alike.

'His antics on TV, just hours after missing a crucial parliamentary vote affecting his constituency [on the Crossrail project], demonstrate that he is becoming one of the biggest laughing stocks in London politics since the Second World War,' said a clearly livid John Biggs, a Labour member of the London Assembly.

Labour Chief Whip Hilary Armstrong, who had launched a petition against Galloway urging him to 'represent and respect his constituents, not further his own ego, as he is by remaining totally out of touch in the *Big Brother* house', was equally furious. 'It made me cringe,' she said of Galloway's feline impersonation. 'I'm absolutely bemused that he decided to do something where he is uncontactable by the people he represents or works for. Something serious could happen here today and no one can contact him, he could not say or do anything – and that to me seems a bit strange for someone who is, and has wanted to be, a publicly elected official.'

It is no exaggeration to say that the whole fiasco could well have been behind Galloway's subsequent decision to stand down as an MP. He had declared on entering the *Big Brother* house that he was doing so to make politics more accessible to the man on the street, but like many an ego before him – Germaine

Greer's brief sojourn in the house springs to mind – he hadn't realised the programme makers would manipulate the situation to their own ends. He was not allowed to talk about politics on air, as there was no one from any other party to get their own point across, and broadcasting rules demanded that Galloway and Respect could not hog the time available. The result was that he was looking as puerile and shallow as the fellow contestants he had been slagging off.

His spokesman tried to play down the furore, saying that the constituency office was open for business and that there was no harm in Galloway's appearing on the show. 'It is his hope that *Big Brother* would provide the kind of platform that the media does not normally provide for him,' he said. 'He is coming across as a human being, while the press have tried to demonise him in the past.'

But it was too late: the damage was done. Rula looked a bit silly, but that was all. Galloway, however, had lost his dignity and, once that happens to a politician, as so many have found out to their cost, there is no going back. And how ironic that his party was called Respect. In the wake of his performance, Galloway was being accorded anything but that. 'When he pretended to be a cat licking cream from Rula's hands, something died inside me,' wrote one commentator, surely speaking for the nation.

Meanwhile, Dennis continued to woo Faria, now bringing up the subject of You Know What. What had really happened with Sven? he asked. It had the potential for a juicy encounter, but turned out to be more of what everyone had heard before. 'I had a relationship with an England coach,' she said. 'He told me, "I don't have a partner. I don't love her." If truth be told, it was just a repetition of an old tale.

With all this going on, Chantelle was proving a breath of fresh air. Asked to try speaking Japanese, she said, 'Oui.' She then remarked that she was tired because, 'I've been up learning German all night.' It might not have had a great deal to do with reality, but, after the bullying of Jodie, the bitchiness of Pete and the cat episode, it was very refreshing.

Elsewhere in the house, there were the usual crises. Faria, Pete and Dennis had all failed in their scientific tasks, which meant that they were to have only £1 per head each day for food and no alcohol. 'With this budget, we're not going to have enough for alcohol and cigarettes,' Jodie said gloomily. But her plight was nearly at an end.

The time had come to evict the first contestant and, to no one's surprise, that person turned out to be

Jodie. It was probably as well for her that her experience was at last at an end. She'd had an awful time, as she related to Davina McCall when she left the house: 'The whole time I was there, I was miserable or defending myself,' she told the show's presenter. 'I was getting it from every angle. I do not think the true me has been shown.' Asked what the show had taught her about herself, she replied, 'That I do not get on with people that pretend they are not transvestites when they really are, that I do not get on with people who tell me I need psychiatric help when they do.' She could barely contain her relief to be out.

With Jodie gone, the house became visibly more relaxed and there was even a degree of hilarity. In yet another new twist to the proceedings, the housemates were about to have a visitor from outside, one who would certainly inject some entertainment into the show. The introduction of Sir Jimmy Savile into the mix, albeit fleetingly, was another inspired idea from the producers. Few entertainers in Britain could be relied upon to lift the spirits like he could, and few could have carried off their appearance with such ease. The presence of the veteran 79-year-old DJ brought a burst of energy to the house and a different atmosphere. He enlivened the daily routine for the housemates, while giving the viewers something to talk about. And he made everyone, inside and outside the house, sit up and take notice.

Sir Jimmy was in high spirits as he arrived, wearing his trademark red tracksuit and with cigars and several tins of baked beans tucked under his arm. 'A good Royal Marine always travels equipped,' he said. 'I have a violent nature, but you have nothing to fear from me,' he told Dennis Rodman as he shook the smouldering American's hand. 'I'm here because I thought you might need something fixing.'

'I've got an earring that needs fixing,' piped up Chantelle.

'You feel good?' asked Barrymore, pumping the newcomer's hand enthusiastically.

'Indestructible,' Sir Jimmy replied.

Once installed in the house, he was as ebullient as ever, excusing the briefness of his visit with typical panache. 'A red-blooded man like me can't stay here overnight with girls like you in here – I'd get three months in the slammer,' he said, to general delight.

The assembled celebs had been asked to give Sir Jimmy a list of their wishes. George Galloway wanted to attend the Oscars 'with the one I love'. Barrymore wanted to try an aircraft simulator, asking, 'Dear Jim, please can you fix it for me to fly an airline simulator and land a jumbo jet at

Heathrow?' Preston wanted to appear in an episode of *EastEnders* and Pete wanted to spend some time with his boyfriend. Chantelle wanted to be a pop star, while Rula wanted to 'provide pleasure for each of the other housemates', a wish that was granted when Sir Jimmy doled out goodie bags full of mugs, badges, an outfit, wig and jewellery.

Then he left, promising to fulfil some – but not all – of the wishes once the celebs were once safely on the outside once more. George was to attend the Baftas. Barrymore was to get his simulated flight. There were talks about Preston appearing on *EastEnders*, while Maggot, who had asked for a classic comedy film to be shown in the *Big Brother* house, was disappointed, receiving instead a compilation tape of the best bits from *Jim'll Fix It*. As for Pete on Sir Jimmy – 'I thought he'd been dead for 15 years, and I've still got no reason to suspect otherwise,' he remarked waspishly.

Sir Jimmy's appearance came after some bizarre tasks had been allocated to the housemates. Earlier that day, they were asked to stay in a selection of cardboard boxes for as long as possible. In order to help them to accomplish this, the producers had given each of them a little survival kit containing a water flask, cake, compass, torch, disposable camera and flag. If they had reckoned on this hyperactive crew being unable to stay still for long, they were quite right.

'It's tiny!' shrieked Chantelle, once inside her box.

'What do we take pictures of?' wondered Rula.

Barrymore could hardly settle at all, while Pete and Preston were first out of their boxes.

Rula managed 52 minutes, for which she received a special pair of beige 'pants of power'. Big Brother instructed her to wear them at all times in order to benefit from special powers during the next round of nominations, scheduled for the following day.

Outside the house, Jodie was relating her tale. It had been a less than happy time for her and she was keen to convey her experiences to the outside world, particularly what she thought about the men in the house. 'Out of all of them, Preston was the only one who was my type,' she revealed. Could this have been why, despite their friendliness on the show, Chantelle distanced herself from Jodie when she came out?

'He had a girlfriend, so I just wouldn't have gone there,' Jodie explained. 'But I wouldn't have done anything more than have a snog on TV because I'm not a porn star. I didn't snog Chantelle in the house but I would've liked to. I snog all my mates, so who knows what will happen when we're out in Essex?'

Precisely nothing, was the answer, but at least it made good copy.

It was Barrymore, however, that Jodie really had issues with. He had torn into her on a number of occasions, and she was determined to tell the world what she thought about him. 'He has got serious, serious issues but he tried to tell me I had serious issues,' she protested. 'I tried to be nice to him but I think he needs help. One day I was sitting on a chair and Michael said, "You're only sitting there because there's a camera on you." I said, "You're fucking kidding me, aren't you? The whole house is full of cameras. You're nuts. You can't get away from the cameras, that's the whole point." I never want to see him for the rest of my life.'

Even so, she did have some advice for him: to be completely open with other housemates about the tragedy of Stuart Lubbock's death.

'If I was him, I would have to have brought it up the minute I walked in – because I'd know that everyone was thinking about it,' she said. 'Every single person thought it as soon as they saw him. Even Chantelle was stressing the other day after she said, "Coming swimming, Michael?" If I was Michael, I would have just said, "Right, let's clear this up. I didn't kill anyone," or whatever.'

While Jodie felt that Barrymore was her main

tormentor, he was by no means the only one. 'The whole thing was hideous. It got to the point where I really didn't know how much more I could take – people were just being so nasty to me. I really did feel bullied. At first, it was just by Michael, Pete and George, then some others jumped on the bandwagon. I hope nobody ever has to go through what I went through in there. I know it doesn't look as bad on screen as it feels when you're actually in the house.

'I've been bullied before, so I knew how to deal with it, but nothing is worth that. My personal happiness is more important than a TV show. I kept saying in the Diary Room that if those three hadn't been in there I would have had a whale of a time. Everything I did they picked up on.

Not only had Jodie hated the experience, but also it had made for some highly uncomfortable viewing. Quite a few people felt that, for all her personal failings, the way she was treated by the others was downright cruel and, while the show is happy to make life difficult for the housemates, outright cruelty is another matter altogether. Nor had Jodie done herself any favours. She had been keen for viewers to see beyond the slightly tawdry image, but she had not come across at all well, and talking so explicitly about intimate matters was a big mistake.

Back in the house, they were talking about the day that John Lennon died, when suddenly Maggot burst into tears and fled the room, followed by Rula, looking concerned. 'There is someone really close to me,' the poor guy sobbed. 'I don't want to mention her because she doesn't want anything to do with what I'm doing. I think this has got something to do with that.'

Was it his girlfriend? asked Rula.

'Sort of,' Maggot replied, before adding, 'This has taken me by surprise.'

It was obvious that what was really wrong was that he had been missing her and in the present hothouse atmosphere it had just all got too much. Indeed, the oppressive atmosphere provoked unwise behaviour among a number of the housemates over the course of their stay, especially George Galloway, but more about that later.

At this point, Chantelle and Preston were joint favourites to win the show, with odds of 2/1. Maggot was 5/1, Pete Burns 10/1 and Faria Alam the outsider at 50/1. Pete was tipped to leave next. He was 2/1 favourite to become the second celeb out in the next eviction, on Wednesday. The country remained gripped and, while there was a strong contingent that absolutely loathed the man, he also had a surprisingly high number of fans. He could be absolutely savage, but his ferocious wit couldn't help but entertain most of those around him, and a lot of people on the outside as well.

By now, another development was becoming apparent even to the casual observer. The housemates had been in situ for a week and it looked as if Preston was beginning to take more than a passing interest in Chantelle. Following a party held for Traci, Preston's inhibitions seemed decidedly loosened and after gazing at Chantelle for some time he started chasing her round the house. He then demanded (and received) a foot massage, before applying himself to tickling her. 'Chantelle,' he announced, 'if I didn't have a girlfriend, I'd marry you in a minute.'

'And I'd marry you, too,' Chantelle replied.

'That is sooooooo sweet, I can't take it!' declared Traci, before a flurry of teasing from everyone else about who would be bridesmaids forced Chantelle to retreat in embarrassment.

It is difficult to know if the two of them were being serious back then, but joking often has a serious side to it and this was the first indication of a serious mutual attraction. And that was not the end of it. Shortly afterwards, Preston was seen wooing Chantelle with the assurance, 'As long as you and me are both in here, it will be OK.'

On the outside, it seemed she had another admirer – none other than Jodie, who had confessed she would like to have a romp with Chantelle. Doubtless emboldened by her freedom, she was able to say at last what she really felt about some of the others. 'Dennis tried to grab my crotch about three times,' she revealed. 'I felt invaded by him. He was sexually aggressive. He'd grab me from behind and push me over and push himself into me. He'd get me in a headlock and whisper to me that he was going to have me. Dennis asked me to sleep with him over and over again. At first, I thought he was doing it just to me and Chantelle, but then I realised he was doing it to Faria and Rula. And he was even being like that with Pete as well. He and Pete were making sexual innuendoes all the time.'

Unsurprisingly, Barrymore also came in for some of her anger. 'That man makes me feel sick,' Jodie said. 'I was talking about losing Kim [Baynard, a friend of hers who had been murdered three years previously] and how sad I felt. Instead of being normal, he had to be evil and screamed, "I've lost someone – I lost my wife." Wait a minute, isn't that the wife he left for another man? I know people saw me having big mood swings in the house, but viewers haven't seen the real Barrymore. Let me tell you, he was a man on the edge. A lot of the time he mumbles and he comes out with sentences that just don't make sense.'

George Galloway didn't fare much better. 'I was appalled that he came into the house,' said an indignant Jodie. 'What's an MP doing in there? He's a vile little man who has claimed that he's a devoted father. I'm young enough to be his daughter but he treated me in the most evil way. Actually, he hardly ever mentioned his daughter, so he probably doesn't know how to treat younger women.' It was a real settling of scores.

Pete Burns, though, drew the harshest words of all. 'He kept going on about how he wanted a cannabis joint the whole time,' recalled Jodie. 'But his comments hurt me because he is of sane mind. He knew that what he said would hurt me and he took pleasure in offending me. But surely it isn't just me who is disgusted by him wearing a coat made out of gorilla fur.'

But there was quite a different tone when it came to Chantelle. Jodie had noticed the growing attraction between the new celeb and Preston, and was happy to join in the speculation about what would happen next. 'I think they will definitely snog,' she predicted. 'But I can't imagine them having any sort of lasting relationship. Chantelle is like me. She loves sex and would talk about it a lot and I don't think he could handle her either.' Jodie went on to speculate that she and Chantelle might do a glamour shoot together, an event that has so far failed to take place.

But Jodie was certainly not the only one to have fallen for the Essex girl's charms. So popular was Chantelle now that she had become the bookie's favourite to win the show. Her odds had been slashed from 16/1 to 13/8, while Rupert Adams of William Hill revealed that one person had placed £4,000 on her to win. 'The money suggests that punters have finally had enough of so-called celebrities and are backing Chantelle to win,' he said. Preston was second, followed by Maggot, with Barrymore and Pete sharing fourth place.

George, meanwhile, continued to be the subject of fierce criticism from outside the house for putting his own pleasure before his parliamentary duties. Oona King, the former Labour MP for Bethnal Green and Bow, who had lost her seat to George at the last general election, commented, 'Personally, I don't disagree with George Galloway going on to *Big Brother* for moral reasons, but I do think there is an issue that he's not there or available to do the hard graft of what being a good constituency MP is all about. For some people, the word "opportunism" would leap to mind – but not me.'

And still rumours of a romance between Chantelle and Preston continued to circulate. In fact, the two were now flirting quite openly. 'Don't you think that everyone's just looking at us, waiting for something to happen?' asked Chantelle coyly.

'We're having a secret affair in here, aren't we?' said Preston.

'Yeah, yeah, blatantly,' said Chantelle, managing to agree with him and contradict him at the same time.

It was Preston's birthday, something that offered further opportunities to the two lovebirds. 'Hey, birthday boy, I was going to kiss you, but only on the cheek,' said Chantelle, who later asked, 'When do you want your ten kisses?'

'Now,' Preston replied.

They were confiding in each other, too. Chantelle told Preston that all her boyfriends had cheated on her and that she'd decided, 'I'd rather be on my own than be with the wrong person.'

'You're in the wrong circles,' Preston advised her. 'I'll invite you out to meet my friends.'

The pair even made it into the same bed – although nothing much took place – after a day of hand-holding to celebrate Preston's birthday, before they finally parted at 2am.

But there was one small problem: Preston already had a girlfriend, Camille, whose feelings as she watched this were not hard to guess. And by now Preston appeared to be having the odd twinge of conscience. At one point, he informed Faria, 'It's just turned into something when it's nothing,' and on another occasion he asked Pete, who had expressed a desire to leave the house during the next round of nominations, 'When you leave, can you see my girlfriend and explain?'

But almost immediately afterwards he was pining for Chantelle again. 'I just think she's lovely,' he said. 'Not in a way like that. I just think she's adorable, like a little doll. I was going to say I just want to play with her. But not like that. She's adorable. I just wanna grab her cheeks and go, Whoooooo! I think last night I was a bit pissed. I do like her. I get a bit touchy-feely when I drink. No, I'm not going to let this be a big thing. I'm not worried. [To Chantelle] I think we were smooching a bit yesterday.'

'What?' replied Chantelle. 'No we weren't. Preston, we didn't kiss at all. Nothing happened.'

'You were kissy-kissy, huggy-huggy,' Traci chipped in.

It did nothing to calm matters down when, shortly afterwards, Preston was seen slipping a ring on Chantelle's finger, even if he was doing it in jest. Chantelle promptly hugged him and showed off her ring, before confessing, 'We tried to keep away from each other, but that only makes it worse, because it looks as if you're trying to hide something.'

If they were trying, they weren't succeeding that well. In the Diary Room, Preston said of Chantelle, 'If she left before me, I'd be devastated.'

Back with her again, he told her, 'You have all the qualities I find in people I love. I feel like I'm ten years old. We clicked straight away.'

'Ditto,' she replied.

It would be nice to say that the other housemates applauded the romance that was budding before their eyes. Nice, but totally inaccurate. For whatever reason, the growing intimacy between the two, who by now were taking strolls around the garden together, seemed to act as a severe irritant to the others, especially Pete. 'What the hell are they doing?' he demanded. 'What are they on? She's a pop tart and she's playing to the cheap seats.'

'They have to stop it now. How naive can they be?' demanded Barrymore.

'They'll track down Preston's girlfriend and ask her what she thinks about it all,' said Faria, who knew a fair bit about how the press react when they are interested in someone's romantic life.

Dennis offered Preston a fatherly warning: 'Last night I was thinking, this kid's gonna regret this shit tomorrow.'

Chantelle herself began to worry about how they appeared, telling her beau, 'We'd better not be alone together, if you know what I mean.'

With perfect timing, an interview with Preston hit the newsstands in which he talked about his relationships, saying the first encounter came during a game of Spin the Bottle. 'I don't want to think about it. It's a bit skivvy,' he said, before confessing that he had lost his virginity at 13. He was not, however, a womaniser. 'I'm massively un-rock 'n' roll when it comes to that,' he said. 'I'm all about having a girlfriend, watching telly and drinking wine rather than having an awkward fumble with a stranger.' And on the subject of ending relationships? Like so many men, Preston was not that good at giving someone the old heave-ho. 'You pretend you're depressed and need time alone, when really you fancy someone else,' he admitted.

Viewers' attention was temporarily diverted from this innocent affair when another row broke out as the next round of nominations reared its ugly head. Getting into matters perhaps best left untouched on a show like *Big Brother*, Faria, who'd heard that she was one of the nominees to leave, caused uproar by claiming that the British public would not let anyone win the show who wasn't white. 'Do you think they'll ever let a black or Asian girl or guy win this thing?' she said to Traci and Dennis. 'Are you out of your tree? Think about it, darling. Never. Remember that. This country? Oh, please! Don't even get me going on that. They would never, they'd be up in fucking arms.'

If this was meant to be a passing jibe, almost immediately to be forgotten, it soon proved anything but. For a start, Traci, who has African-American, Native American and Italian blood in her veins, was outraged. 'For me, I thought it was going to be fair and square... I thought I did have a chance to win,' she said as she recounted the conversation to the others. 'But, according to Faria and Dennis, because I'm female and I'm American and my skin is brown, I don't stand a chance.'

Putting forward another point of view, George fumed, 'The idea that people who watch this show are bigots is preposterous. Most of the people who've won have been from minorities of one kind or another.'

'The idea of anybody putting that into their vote in the house is an insult,' added Rula.

And, if that were not enough, Dennis then got upset because it had been implied that he had made the remarks, rather than Faria. So heated did the situation become that Faria was forced to apologise to Dennis, to the nation – in fact, to pretty much everyone. 'Traci had misunderstood and said that Dennis had said something when it was actually I who had said it,' she began.

'I said, and I didn't refer to anybody here, that I didn't think it was possible for a black or an Asian to win *Big Brother*. But I didn't mention the "r" word, I meant it just as that. Then Dennis agreed and I said, "Why are you here?" and he said, "To add colour." I assumed he was talking about skin colour and he wasn't, he was talking about adding spice and entertainment. So it was me, I said that, and it wasn't him. It had nothing to do with anybody inside who had said anything.'

What really appeared to be wrong was hurt feelings. Faria had, after all, been nominated to leave the house, and it seemed to be this that was really upsetting her. She was in tears as she continued, 'I do feel a little hurt that I've been nominated but I'm sorry but I just do. I'm sorry if I get upset but I've tried to be who I am. I apologise to the nation, to everybody here for offending. Obviously, this will cause a lot of aggravation but I've got to take it on the chin.'

Perhaps affected by the mood of apology, Traci also said sorry. 'I guess it looked like Dennis was the big bad guy and he's not,' she said.

Later, when tempers had cooled, Faria talked to

Traci about what she'd really meant. 'I said what I had to say. Maybe it was wrong or whatever. I stuck my neck out. That's cool. That's fine. I know who nominated me, that's fine. I'm hurt by it because I'm a bit surprised. I also knew I would be out after Jodie. I wasn't shocked. Just a bit surprised. I was a bit emotional. I shut everybody up when I said what I said in there.'

5

Will They, Won't They?

The people who had voted to expel Faria turned out to be George, Maggot and Barrymore. Dennis was also on the receiving end of three votes, from Faria, Chantelle and Preston. Chantelle's verdict: he was 'really crafty' and 'I can't have a drink without him watching'. Her feelings didn't go unnoticed, for Dennis in turn had nominated her 'because she's a kid, she's kind of lost there, she's overwhelmed', an analysis that was to prove very wide of the mark. He nominated Rula, too, because she 'emotionally broke down'.

The mood of recrimination was general. Faria had chosen Pete, who, she said in something of an understatement, 'can be quite crass and vulgar', and Dennis, 'a bit of a dark horse' who enjoyed 'provoking me for nothing'. George nominated Traci, for not being talkative enough, and Faria. 'I think she's ill and depressed,' he said, pulling no punches. 'She feels out of her depth, doesn't really have much to say. She is, after all, famous for only one thing... I think she feels that she doesn't have anything to say about showbusiness, music, politics... she feels adrift.'

They were all at it now. Barrymore's reason for nominating Faria was that 'she really struggles with the dynamics and the crowd of us in here. [She is] a people pleaser, just telling people what they want to hear.' And Maggot remarked pointedly that Faria 'spoke to me in a certain way that I didn't like... I wasn't pleased to be patronised in the way I was.'

And so it went on. Pete on Rula: 'She thinks I'm gross, vulgar, trashy.' And on Chantelle: 'She hasn't done anything, she just bluffed her way into celebrity status.' Preston on Traci: 'She's finding it hard to keep that act up [her sunny outlook] for so long. So the only way is to be silent, sit in the sauna and change outfits 20 times a day.' Traci on George: 'I feel like he personally offended me in a major way with his opinions.' Traci on Michael: 'He hoards the kitchen.' And Rula, whose 'pants of power' allowed her to nominate a third candidate, on Pete: 'He's very high-maintenance and, although the most colourful member of the house, very unpredictable.'

You could say that again. But with everyone's ego now enjoying free rein, it was a miracle that the household stayed as calm as it did. Chantelle was still the favourite to win, not least because her slightly dingbat pronouncements were actually going down very well in the outside world. The most recent was apropos Dennis: '[He] says he's slept with two thousand women. That's more than a hundred. That's more than five hundred!' There was no arguing with that, and saying it just made the world love Chantelle all the more.

Even the bickering soon became more amicable. When the celebs were asked by Big Brother to paint a self-portrait, for which they were to be rewarded with alcohol, cigarettes and cigars, a certain jocularity took hold of the place again. Dennis got Chantelle to paint his nails pink, before giving Barrymore a slap on the bum. 'He really loves you, then,' said a wry George when Barrymore related the tale to him.

When Barrymore reproached the others for not thanking him for all the time he was spending in the kitchen, remarking, 'You'll notice the prison bitch doesn't get a hug,' he was rewarded with an embrace from Traci.

Then there was his quick spat with Dennis, who described the show as 'only TV shit'.

'What's your shit?' demanded Barrymore, who had made his name on the box. 'I don't get involved with your basketball shit. Why are you getting involved with this TV shit?'

Dennis replied that he did not want to argue, adding, 'I'm not threatening you – yet.'

Pete continued to bitch. Chantelle, he said, 'was as dim as a string of fairy lights'. If this was an attempt to get the public on board, it failed. They quite clearly adored her, and the blossoming romance with Preston merely added to her charm. When she got tipsy, it merely inspired more affection from outside the house, particularly when she decided to give up drinking – at least for the rest of the evening. Then came the revelation that she thought Dundee was in Wales. It all went down a treat. She was beginning to be spoken of as the next Jade Goody, which is, after all, quite a compliment: Jade is by far the most successful contestant to have appeared on *Big Brother* so far.

But, understandably, her blossoming romance was not going down well in one quarter. For Camille, it was a horrible time: not only was her fiancé – it had emerged that she and Preston were engaged – clearly falling for someone else, but he was doing it on national television and there was no way she could talk to him. The strain was beginning to tell. Colleagues at her workplace, Virtusales, in the Hove Technology Centre, spoke of their concern. 'She arrived in a state and spent the morning on the phone to pals,' said one. 'She was also speaking in French to her family. Just after lunch, it all got too much and she asked to go home early. She's in absolute turmoil.'

More details began to emerge about Preston's relationship with Camille Aznar. Camille, now 25, first met Preston at a gig in Nottingham after she came to study in England, and the couple had been together a year. Both lived in Hove, East Sussex, near the St Patrick's Trust homeless charity, to which Preston had pledged to donate money from his fee for the show. Brunette and sophisticated, Camille was said to be very different from her love rival.

'Camille is gorgeous and charming and very clever – the complete opposite of Chantelle,' said Preston's band mate James Gregory. 'She was planning something for him when he gets out, if you know what I mean. So my advice to Preston right now is: "Just remember you've got a girlfriend" – that's all I can say. Right now, Camille definitely needs to hear that he loves her. You have got to imagine what you would be feeling if it was your partner. It's awkward to see because he probably does have some feelings for Chantelle.' James was too right there. Just how those feelings would develop would shortly become clear.

As expected, Faria was the next to go. She departed with a certain amount of dignity – not easy, since, like Jodie, she had to undergo a chorus of boos, and seemed, on the whole, relieved to be out. The others, meanwhile, were getting on with the next chores and tasks set by Big Brother. Harmony reigned, if briefly.

And that was remarkable, given the amount Big Brother was doing to unsettle the little tribe. George and Preston were called to the Diary Room to be reprimanded for discussing nominations, and as a punishment were told that they had to agree on three people to be nominated for eviction. These three were Traci, Maggot and Rula, the last rather surprisingly, given how well she'd been getting on with George. Chantelle, needless to say, was not on the list.

As they left, George muttered to Preston, 'We'll just tell them we've been punished, but not what we had to do.' What they didn't know, of course, was that the rest of the house had been watching them in the Diary Room. The others were remarkably sanguine, though, agreeing that it was 'all part of the game'.

It was around this point that George began to realise he might have made a serious mistake in agreeing to participate in the show. For the first time, he began to sense that something in the wider world might be amiss after he was beamed from the house to make an appearance on *Richard and Judy*, his first contact in over a week with the great outside. Afterwards, he seemed genuinely worried as he reported to the celebs, 'Richard and Judy gave the impression there is enormous interest in the show. And trouble.'

'What do you mean trouble?' asked Chantelle.

'They said, "We can't tell you what the papers, public or the MPs have been saying." So the MPs must have been attacking me for being here.'

'Or congratulating you for coming in,' said Rula.

'No, I think it's attacking,' said George, getting up to go for a walk round the garden. And he was right.

But the house didn't stay sanguine for long. It was nominations time again, which always brought out the worst in all of them, especially Pete. 'I'd be relieved if Rula went,' he announced. 'I don't share any common ground or humour with her and that fucking booming voice of hers gets on my nerves.' Then, recalling when Rula had got locked in the loo, he really went on the attack. 'Oh dear, what can the matter be, clapped-out actress locked in the lavatory…'

Rula, although unaware of this most recent slight, came out of the bedroom looking concerned. 'I woke up with a start, thinking it was morning,' she said, as Pete pulled faces behind her head in an attempt to distract Barrymore. 'Probably something to do with eviction day,' she went on. 'I'm prepared for it, I think. If it's meant to be...'

Meanwhile, the flirting between Preston and Chantelle was intensifying. He was caught stroking her bum. 'I love Chantelle more than she probably thinks I do,' he told Rula, after which the smitten couple ended up cuddling in bed again.

'You were so hot,' said Chantelle. 'I can't resist. Marry me now!'

Pete, who had a great deal more common sense than his appearance would suggest, stepped in. 'I don't think your girlfriend will be happy,' he said. 'It's on TV. It's humiliation.'

'I'm a horrendous flirt,' Preston replied.

He had not, of course, forgotten he had a girlfriend on the outside, and nor had Chantelle. His enthusiasm for Chantelle kept being tempered with bouts of guilt about Camille, leading Chantelle to say to him the next morning, 'You didn't wake up in bed with me, we haven't snogged, we haven't had a fumble in the dark. You shouldn't have a guilty conscience, you've done nothing wrong.' But that wasn't the way Camille saw it. She had let it be known that she was no longer watching the show, and who could blame her? Preston might still have been nominally with her, but it was obvious that he was increasingly drawn to Chantelle. And it was all taking place live in front of millions.

The other housemates refrained from commenting on the relationship growing ever stronger under their noses, pursuing instead their usual regime of backstabbing and attempting to be the centre of attention, with a little innocuous conversation thrown in for good measure. In fact, Maggot had not even been paying attention to what had been going on. 'I have a heavy hungover feeling,' he complained in the morning. 'I'm still a bit perplexed as to the reasons I was nominated. I didn't realise Preston was so much into Chantelle.'

George, meanwhile, was living down to his reputation by turning on his erstwhile mate Rula. 'She has the same thespian insincerity as LA insincerity,' he announced. 'I liked her at first but I soon went off her.' Not a very gallant turn of phrase for a self-confessed ladies' man, and, as Rula was the next to leave, she was able to say so herself, blasting him for his two-faced behaviour.

Inevitably, one person who had been watching the closeness developing between Chantelle and

Preston was Chantelle's mother, Vivien. Ever since her daughter had arrived in the *Big Brother* house, there had been a good deal of interest in the Houghton family, and now Vivien herself appeared on the box, courtesy of Richard and Judy, to say what she thought about it all. 'Everyone in there is a bit crazy apart from Preston,' she confided. 'He has been pretty down-to-earth and normal and they bounce off each other. But I don't know if she fancies him or not.'

The conversation turned to Pete, by far the most outspoken of the oddly assorted group. Vivien was not worried about him verbally savaging her daughter. 'I think Chantelle can stand up to him,' she said.

Another of Richard and Judy's guests had his own view of the man. 'The thing about Pete that is interesting is that he is almost talking to himself,' said the music journalist Paul Morley. 'In a bunch of quite weak and vulnerable characters, he may turn out to be the most vulnerable.' If Morley was right, it was certainly a quality Pete was keeping well hidden for now.

With Chantelle herself still locked away from reality in the house, Vivien was having to deal with business proposals for her daughter without being able to consult her. For a start, a singing career seemed to be on the cards: Fat Fox Music had secured the rights for 'I Want It Right Now', a song originally written for Kylie Minogue by Paul Bell and Colin Campsie, laid down a backing track and were hoping to get Chantelle into a studio to record the number for real as soon as she came out. She had certainly enjoyed singing in front of the housemates, saying, 'That was wicked. It gave me the biggest buzz.'

Now she was attracting attention inside the house from someone other than Preston. Dennis and Faria had been flirting together, but, with Faria gone, Dennis had turned his attentions to Chantelle, asking her if she needed help in the shower. Preston was not present as he did so, which was probably just as well.

A crisis blew up: Chantelle was running low on make-up.

'This is getting serious,' declared Preston. 'I don't think it's funny. Imagine how much I use. My skin goes into shock if there isn't make-up on it.'

'I go into shock,' agreed Chantelle, as she confessed to using a mix of Traci and Pete's supplies. 'Does my face look extra brown?'

'Yes,' said Preston rather ungallantly. 'You look stupid. You look bright orange.'

'You've been Tangoed,' said Maggot.

'If it's the choice between being Tangoed and looking like a dead trout…' Chantelle replied.

And still the 'will they, won't they?' saga went on.

Outside the house, the next person to step into the fray was Preston's sister, Louie, two years his junior. Camille confided in her, saying, 'It's very tough watching Preston and Chantelle. But I'll be waiting for him when he comes out of the house to hear what he has to say. He is my boyfriend, after all. I know how it may look but I am convinced Preston's relationship with Chantelle is more affection than attraction. It's so hard not being able to speak to him or reach out to him.'

She was being extremely brave, and at this stage there was still no real indication of what Preston would eventually do. In fact, he didn't seem to know himself. Louie, for her part, seemed to think that Camille was right. 'Camille is a very independent, intelligent and mature woman,' she said. 'Preston often acts affectionately – like he does with Chantelle – after a few drinks. He's always hugging pals on nights out. He's a bit of a softie.'

He was also clearly a very loving older brother. This situation between him and Chantelle was not just provoking interest in the young lady; he was also benefiting from a great deal of attention. It emerged that his parents had parted in 1998, a split that resulted in his mother Miranda, a US citizen, returning to the States, while his father Anthony worked away from home as a stuntman. This meant that Preston, who had been a child actor and had starred with Elizabeth Hurley in the BBC drama *Christabel* – one of the very few roles for which the actress received rave reviews – had to look after his younger sister while still a teenager himself.

'I know that is why we are so close, because we had to go through something that is really, really tough,' said Louie. 'It was just Preston and me. Our oldest brother, Alex, was at university. I couldn't have got through it without Preston. He was only two years older but he was there for me one hundred per cent. He made sure I went to school and looked presentable. And, when I was down, he knew just what to say to make me feel better. Preston always made sure I didn't go off the rails. I was only 14 and could have gone wild. If I went out with an idiot, Preston would say to me, "You are not going out with him – you deserve better." He still says it now!'

It must be said that Preston's behaviour towards his sister showed a truly decent side to his character. He and his band the Ordinary Boys had signed a six-figure record deal in 2004, but he always made sure he was around to see that Louie was all right. The following year he threw a twenty-first birthday party for her, complete with a giant chocolate cake. And Louie was the first person he rang when he knew he was going to be doing *Big Brother*. 'Preston and I have always been big fans of the show,' she said. 'He called me first because he knew I'd support him.'

Back in the house, the next round of nominations for eviction came up and, rather to everyone's surprise, Chantelle was on the list, alongside George and Dennis. It was the first time her name had come up – she'd been nominated by Dennis, Pete and Traci – and one person looked absolutely horrified: Preston. Pete was his usual frank self about why he'd nominated her. 'She's been playing dumb and dumber and giggly and gigglier in a bid to win,' he snapped.

Chantelle took the news with aplomb. 'This is exciting, means my foundation [her make-up, that is] problems isn't a problem, got less time for it to last. This makes me feel a little bit happier about the foundation situation. I guess I'll be seeing my mum soon. I am gonna cry my eyes out when I see her. I really miss her.' It was a typically Chantelle-esque way of handling unwelcome news.

As for the others, intimations of trouble for George intensified. After his housemates were shown a video clip of him discussing them with Rula, they rose up as one and banned him from voting in this particular round. He might have prided himself on his *savoir-faire*, but he looked pretty grim-faced as the nominations started coming in. 'He's shifty, really crafty, a bit smarmy,' said Chantelle as she voted for him.

Maggot agreed. 'I think it's about time he went back,' he said. 'I think his constituents deserve to have him back where he belongs. If he's gonna continue breaking the rules, it doesn't help life in here.'

In a sure sign that feelings were running high about him inside the house as well as outside, Traci also cast her vote for George. 'He is extremely two-faced, offensive, confusing,' she said. 'He feels this way about me, but doesn't have the balls to say it to my face.'

The games continued. The housemates were forced to don leotards – 'I wouldn't run from a burning building wearing this,' said Pete as he donned a turquoise number – and perform dances to express a range of emotions in various dancing styles. This was another moment that was to come back and haunt a scarlet-clad Galloway, who was required to express bewilderment through robotic movements. A prescient Maggot said, 'This has complications for him outside, as people think, What the fuck are you doing?' Chantelle, paired with Barrymore, managed quite well, or humorously at least, to convey rage through Irish dancing.

Another task was set, one calculated to confuse just about everybody. Chantelle was made director of the Big Brother Bank: she chose Preston as her fellow director, while the six remaining housemates became bankers. The rules were too complicated to repeat here, but essentially Chantelle and Preston thought everyone had to pass a certain number of tasks, whereas in fact everyone had to fail them. Of course, this merely succeeded in bringing the two of them even closer together, not least because they were closeted in a mock-up of a private members' club, a luxury room complete with roaring fire and portraits of the two on the wall, and fed whisky, chocolates and strawberries. 'George will be gutted,' said Chantelle. The 'will they, won't they?' debate became more intense still, with Pete adding his own unique take on it by calling Preston a whore and Chantelle a liar.

Chantelle was too right about George. Already livid that the others had not allowed him to vote in the last round of nominations, and with his ego badly dented by the fact that a fair few of them wanted him out, he allowed his suave demeanour to finally snap. For starters, he rounded on Preston and Chantelle for wining and dining in their private club, while the rest of the housemates went without. It was a trivial thing to get upset about, but the group had been existing in a hothouse, cut off from the outside world for some time now, and tempers were clearly fraying.

'If I'd been called in there, I would have stood ramrod straight, refused to sit down, refused to eat, refused to drink, refused to smoke. I would have said, "You brought me here under duress, but I will refuse to partake in things that the others are not allowed,"' he declaimed, perhaps forgetting that he was in the *Big Brother* house and not addressing the US Senate.

'We were playing a game,' said Chantelle, slightly irritated. 'Are you saying you wouldn't have had any of that stuff?'

'I would not!' Galloway replied.

'Well, I really wish you'd done the task instead of us then,' said Chantelle, quite reasonably wondering what all the fuss was about.

But Galloway was not through yet. The housemates had been watching Chantelle and Preston at their private feast, and he now turned his attentions on the young man. 'You're a sneak and a liar and you're exposed to the world as a sneak and a liar,' he announced, winning no points at all for himself in the process. 'You float around promiscuously – stroking, metaphorically or literally, everybody's ass to protect your own. We saw on the screen your real character portrayed for all to see. And that's my last word.' If only.

The housemates had also banned George from discussing his fellow celebs, and Preston reminded him of this fact. All it did was add fuel to the flames. 'Pipe down, Mr Indignation,' George stormed. 'We'll see what the viewers thought of your double standards, your indignation about me and the aplomb with which you become a lying plutocrat in your gentleman's club.' It was an extraordinary denunciation, for George, who was not averse to the finer things in life himself, was not fighting a class war but taking part in a game on television. It might have been the fact that he was beginning to realise that he'd done himself some lasting harm outside the house that brought on this outburst. But, whatever the reason, it was now Barrymore's turn to feel the Galloway ire.

'You never let anyone speak. Now you're going to let me speak,' the MP snarled. 'I was close to you, Dennis was close to you, and you stabbed both of us over your mania for hoarding cigarettes. You're a real cigarette addict and you ought to address the fact that you've no loyalty to anybody.'

Worse still, in Galloway's eyes, Barrymore had failed to stand up for him when the others decided he shouldn't take part in the last round of nominations. 'You sat shtum and said nothing,' he hissed. 'You care about no one except yourself. You're the most selfish, self-obsessed person I've ever met. I cared a lot about you. You stabbed me in the back.'

'You're going to be sorry for what you said to the kids, and you're going to be sorry for what you started here tonight,' said Barrymore.

'As Rodney King said, can't we all just get along?' Traci piped up.

Galloway had damaged himself irreparably in the eyes of both the group and the outside world. 'George has got problems with everyone right now. He is playing a game and is losing grip of the game and has turned into a bit of a psycho, which is weird,' said Maggot, displaying a wisdom beyond his years. 'George is just attacking anybody right now because he's going to get chucked out in a day or two.'

Preston, calling him a 'school bully', agreed. 'It must be stressful for him now because he knows he's blown it,' he said. 'He will leave here a villain because he cheated and bullied.'

That wasn't the half of it. Galloway now seemed such a dead cert for eviction that William Hill put the odds on him being booted out at 12/1. 'George is one of the shortest-priced favourites we have ever quoted for an eviction, the main reason being that we do not want to take any money on this one,' said Rupert Adams, a spokesman for the company. 'To put it bluntly, we are not a charity.' Rarely had someone fallen so far and so fast on the show.

Meanwhile, interest in Preston continued to build outside the house. A friend of his called Chris, a singer in a rival band called Cat The Dog, painted a rather wild picture of Preston's friends than the one offered by Preston himself. 'We're all stoners to the max,' he declared. 'All Preston's mates are total mash heads. I don't mind admitting I'm a mash head. Everyone in Preston's flat is a mash head.

'He could have his pick of two or three girls a night, and also liked a drink especially after the Ordinary Boys made it big, getting a Top 20 hit in the UK and going straight to number one in Japan. Preston's really been there, if you know what I mean. He lived that rock star life to the full and everyone has continued using his flat as party central but he has really cleaned himself up to go on the TV. He had to sort himself out and he has done.'

In fact, Camille appeared to have done a great deal to calm her boyfriend down. One clever reporter got access to Preston's flat and was shown around the place. 'Come and have a look in his bedroom – you wouldn't believe some of the action that went on in there,' said Preston's friend Andy, another musician. 'He cleaned out most of his stuff before he went into the house and he got himself a steady girlfriend and became really boring, virtually a homosexual – no, just kidding.'

By all accounts, the flat Preston lived in was a typically laddish affair: mess, drink and ashtrays all over the place. One fellow drinker at his local, the Fiddlers Elbow in Brighton, recalled that he did indeed know how to enjoy himself. 'Preston really liked a drink,' he said. 'Then he'd trot the short journey to Ricky Tiks, a trendy late-night bar.' But this did appear to have changed. Preston still liked a drink, as had been evident during the show, but his lifestyle had clearly not got out of hand.

As *Celebrity Big Brother* continued to fascinate the nation, Sir Jimmy Savile popped up to give his own analysis of its appeal. It is well known that, behind all the bombast and the showmanship, Sir Jimmy is a wise and compassionate man, and this came out in what he said about the series. 'I had to be a guest, not a housemate,' he said. 'I wanted nothing to do with evictions and nominations. The reaction was terrific. I had my battle-plan worked out beforehand. If you are going into a fight, always pick on the biggest geezer.

'So that's why I made a beeline for Dennis Rodman. If you lose, at least you're a champion and, if you win, the others knuckle down. So for anyone to walk up to him and say, "Stand up, I have a violent temper but you have nothing to fear from me" was always going to ease tension. He never said a word but he made all sorts of funny growling noises and of course I knew he was thinking, Who the hell is this? But he ended up on my wavelength and saying I was his brother. That's good enough for me.'

Also perceptive was what Sir Jimmy had to say about Chantelle. An enormous amount was being made of her as the typical Essex blonde – cute but dumb, a bit silly really. But what no one had seemed to notice is that not only had she got into the house in the first place, but she was holding her own to such an extent that she was now a favourite to win. Sir Jimmy felt there was rather more going on there than at first met the eye.

'Chantelle is a con artist, in the nicest sense,' he said. 'She's not daft, because she's going to win. It takes one to know one and I know that she's not as dumb as she's portraying. She's a wind-up merchant. When she said to Barrymore, "What do you do?" and he said he was a gynaecologist and she said, "What do they do?", I couldn't believe what I was looking at. But she's lovely with it.' He was, of course, spot on, right down to his prediction that Chantelle would win the show.

Over the previous few days, there had been reports that a furious Camille had returned to France: rather surprisingly, it turned out that she had actually been staying with Preston's elder brother, Alex. Indeed, she went out with their family to celebrate Alex's birthday in London that Saturday night and laughed off reports about what her boyfriend was up to. 'There's no rift with Preston at all,' said a friend. 'It's not nice seeing her boyfriend flirt with someone else. But Camille knows he is just doing what he has to do to win. She accepts he is a loving guy and has always been touchy-feely. She is letting him get on with it – and will be waiting for him when he comes back to the real world.'

As it happened, things looked like they were cooling off between Preston and Chantelle. Both had been warned repeatedly about their behaviour by their housemates, and now Chantelle, at least, appeared to be aware that she might face criticism once she left. Locked inside with Preston and the other celebs, completely cut off from the outside world, she must have felt that Camille somehow did not exist and that therefore Preston really was a single man. But she had begun to see this was not necessarily the case, and, besides, she couldn't have forgotten that the entire country had been following her billing and cooing with Preston 24 hours a day. Her response seemed to be to try to put some distance between them.

As one *Big Brother* source summed it up, 'They have been told by the other celebrities for some time to be careful, but they have been quite inseparable. It may just be because they have more in common with each other than with anyone else in there. It's a tough environment but their flirting is insensitive – and they're finally starting to realise that.'

6

He's Not My Partner

As the days wore on, the housemates continued to veer between bickering, teasing, foul-mouthing one another and just simply attempting to cause trouble. Pete was in his element when it came to stirring it up, and no sooner had he told Chantelle and Preston to cool it than he was trying to get them together again. As Chantelle went off to have a shower, he called out, 'Get in there with her, Preston. Help her shave the back of her legs. It's a nice bonding ritual when your partner gets in and helps you shave your bits.'

'He's not my partner,' said Chantelle a bit uncertainly.

'In here he is,' said Pete. 'He's in the show.'

'I think I'll manage,' said Chantelle, and did a hasty vanishing act.

The housemates were as busy as ever with the tasks they had been set. The latest was a rather bizarre film they were to make about their time in the house, in which they were to play one another. There was ample opportunity for bitchery: Pete donned a large pair of fake breasts to play Jodie, while Chantelle got to be Dennis. In doing so, she swore constantly, something that seemed to irritate him. Traci was Pete, Dennis got to do some cross-dressing to portray Traci, and Michael and George had to be each other. To do this, George put on an apron and cap, while Barrymore pulled some very strange faces. Preston was Rula, for which role he put on a red wig and did some Buddhist chanting. Maggot was the director of the film and played both Chantelle and Preston. Barrymore also stood in for Maggot, while poor old Faria was portrayed by a wig. At the end of the exercise, the housemates were presented with the premiere of *Big Brother: The Movie*.

And finally the world got to see Chantelle and Preston's first kiss, although as first kisses go, it was a rather unusual one. It was, naturally, another of the tasks set by *Big Brother*: Preston had to kiss not just Chantelle but everyone – that is, Pete, Michael, Traci and Maggot – to get cigarettes for the household. He managed it with aplomb. 'It was easy,' he said cheerily. 'Although kissing Maggot was a little bit embarrassing.'

There were also signs, despite Chantelle's recent slight distance, that she and Preston hoped to continue their relationship once out of the house, with her telling him about her mother. 'Wait till you meet her,' she said. 'She's like me times two!' By now their easy familiarity with one another was so established that they appeared more like a long-term couple, rather than two people who had met only a couple of weeks earlier in the very strange circumstances of a reality-television show. The set-up might have been contrived, but the relationship itself was looking increasingly real.

Chantelle's parents continued to plot her career with the expert help of Max Clifford, who was in no doubt that their daughter had the makings of a star and could end up as successful as Jade Goody. 'She has the looks and personality and she's natural – that's what the British public love,' he said. 'She's the only one in there apart from Preston who's natural. She's just being herself. Her mum and dad came to me to see if I could help and I like them. Everyone I've spoken to says Chantelle's a nice person. Jade is the only person to have made a name for themselves out of nothing on leaving that house. It appeals to me that Chantelle went on to the programme pretending to be a celebrity and now she is a celebrity – there's irony there. But Chantelle should be the next Chantelle. You shouldn't try to be the next anyone else. She's someone I would like to help make the most of what she has.'

One career he could definitely see Chantelle doing – with some foresight, as that is exactly what she has done – was as a television presenter. 'It's early days,' he said. 'She's got her five or ten minutes of fame now and maybe we can make it 15 minutes or more. From talking to people in the TV and music business, there's a lot of potential, and I'm hoping we can make the best of what she's done for herself during the show. The word that comes to mind is "natural". She's a natural person and a lot of people in that house are anything but! I think the British public like that and that's one of the reasons she's increasingly popular. The support she's got out there is superb.'

Another possibility, of course, was modelling. Offers had already started to come in and there was the real possibility, for a while at least, that Chantelle could have a very successful career. She would, however, have to be careful. 'She's lovely and a very pretty girl, and she could potentially get involved with all kinds of things in this area,' Clifford said. 'But one of the most important things is to ensure she doesn't make any fundamental mistakes with her choices. After all, this girl's going to be getting a lot of offers. With modelling, protection is as important as promotion for her. She'll have to be very choosy.'

Something else Chantelle would have to be choosy about, of course, was whom she chose to represent her once she was on the outside again. All these decisions were being made without her input: indeed, she had no idea what kind of future was awaiting her on the outside. And nor had she decided who she wanted to be her agent. There was no way any real plans could be made until she had actually left the house.

Another group of people who were very curious about what the future would hold for Chantelle were the makers of *Big Brother*. With the end of the show approaching, there was intensive speculation not only as to what she would do next, but also where the relationship with Preston would go. One person had the brilliant idea of taking them away to spend time together in some glamorous spot, so that they could get to know each other properly. 'This is just the start of their relationship,' said a *Big Brother* source. 'The attention they will get after they are evicted will be massive. So a deal has been done to help them avoid too much intrusion. They'll be taken to an exclusive resort for up to two weeks. It's the perfect place for romance.'

But not everyone was so sanguine about the future. 'Camille is going to rip his fucking knob off,' said Preston's band mate Pete. 'He's dead meat. Chantelle is falling in love with him.'

It certainly looked that way, but then it looked as if Preston was also falling in love with her. Try as they might, it was impossible for the two to conceal the chemistry between them, or the fact that they clearly preferred each other's company to that of anyone else in the house. And there was nowhere for them to hide while all this was going on: every morning the papers were full of further details about what they had just done, how close they were becoming or even the slightest secret glance... And, as the ratings soared, so more people became engrossed in the couple's story and so the ratings soared still further. It was a virtuous circle, for the programme's makers at least.

Someone else who had a smidgen of trouble on his hands was George. As expected, he and Dennis were the next to leave the house – 'What's George's band called?' asked Chantelle shortly before he left – and when George finally exited it was to the biggest chorus of boos so far. Initially, his demeanour was that of a man who thinks he has triumphed, but watching what happened next was almost painful.

He was shown the headlines that had been generated in his stay throughout the house, footage of him dancing in that scarlet leotard and, finally, horribly, the sequence with him and Rula in which he pretended to be a cat. As if that were not enough, Jeremy Paxman, doyen of BBC2 and not usually the sort of person who pops up on Channel 4 reality shows, popped up on screen in the house. 'A lot has happened while you have been incarcerated, Mr Galloway,' drawled Paxo. 'There are several things we would like to ask you about. Whenever you are ready, so are we. With or without your leotard. In the meantime, do you really think it was a good idea to go into the *Big Brother* house?'

George's housemates had been predicting he was in for trouble: they were absolutely right. Not that he understood right away the full implications of what had happened. He couldn't resist yet another go at the others for not allowing him to vote, at times it looked as if he was trying, in vain, to reproduce his glorious encounter with the US Senate. 'I don't usually lose elections and this was a big one,' he remarked. 'I don't know why I was evicted, I think it was because people want me back out on the road. I didn't like having my voting rights taken away – it was like George Bush in Florida taking people's right to vote away. There was a lot of bitterness building up in there; it's like a pressure cooker.' The public was having none of it. George Galloway was in for a very rough ride.

Chantelle's rather disingenuous remark about George's place of work, incidentally, stood up Sir Jimmy Savile's comment that she wasn't half as daft as she looked. In fact, she was quite clever in coming up with comments like that, for she was perfectly well aware that George was an MP. Another time, after she had been on the receiving end of one of his rants, she came out with the seemingly uncharacteristic comment: 'I can't believe George would bully us – he's just a cheating, conniving, vile little man. He can't get respect from anyone. His party Respect should have three more letters – d, i, s – in front of it.'

And no one was happier than Preston that Chantelle herself had not been one of the duo to leave the house. Early, the next morning he leaped out of his bed and into Chantelle's, before getting up again to dance her round the bedroom crying, 'You're still here!'

None of this did anything whatsoever to dampen Chantelle's popularity with the public and that was important now that the final stage of the show was finally here. It had been going for 23 days, the longest time ever for the celebrity version, and, while the housemates all wanted to win as keenly as ever, their relief at finally being set free was palpable. But so was the anticipation about what would happen next, and that applied to the various relationships within the household as much as anything else. Chantelle had told Traci that she had been seeing someone briefly before the show began, but that it wasn't serious, which meant, of course, that she was totally free to start a new relationship.

Traci had mixed feelings about Preston and Chantelle, at one point saying, 'How can they sit there being all happy if there is another girl involved? A person can't be that cruel.' Later, however, she was sympathetic to the lovebirds, saying, 'You two are so happy and adorable. If you two get married, I really wanna be there.'

George, watching the proceedings from outside, observed, 'Chantelle hopes for something with Preston. But, as for him, who can tell?'

Dennis was also in no mood to be gracious, having realised quite how much positive coverage – and interest – Chantelle had garnered while she was in the house. He, by contrast, had been the subject of some less than favourable articles, and he didn't look pleased about it. 'Everyone's saying she's a star,' he said sniffily. 'How? She hasn't done anything.'

Oh, but she had. She had invented herself in a way that has scarcely ever been seen on television. She went from being no one to being someone – zero to hero – in the space of less than a month, in the public eye and surrounded by the kind of people who were almost certain to divert the spotlight from her. She stood up to some of the biggest egos and personalities in the country. And she played out a kind of morality tale for our times: what is it, exactly, that makes people famous? Should she have achieved the position she had?

For her appearance on the show sparked not only national interest, but also a national debate. To some people she was an exceptionally fortunate woman who had achieved the ultimate goal in life today – fame. To others her success was inexplicable, a sort of postmodern joke. But, if they were right, no one could agree on the answer to the crucial question: who was the joke on?

The upcoming evictions were bringing out the best and the worst in the housemates. Preston admitted that he hoped he would win, but said that he'd be even happier if Chantelle did so. 'It would be like, "Fuck you" to everyone.' He appeared to be suggesting that he wanted her to win only to undermine the notions about celebrity culture,

fter *Celebrity Big Brother* a whole world of opportunity opened itself to Chantelle,
cluding numerous television opportunities, such as appearing on *Loose Women*.

Above: Promoting *Street Muttz* with ex-*Girlie Show* presenter and regular guest on *Big Brother's Big Mouth*, Sarah Cawood.

Below: With Simon Webbe of pop group *Blue* on Saturday morning television.

ove: Donning a crash helmet for the madness that is *Holly and Stephen's Saturday Showdown*.

low: Having a laugh on ITV's quiz show *Mint*.

Above: A seasoned *Big Brother* pro, Chantelle gets ready to enter the German *BB* hou as the surprise guest.

Below: She wasted no time crossing the language barrier and winning over the German housemates.

hantelle dresses as her 'celebrity double' – Paris Hilton.

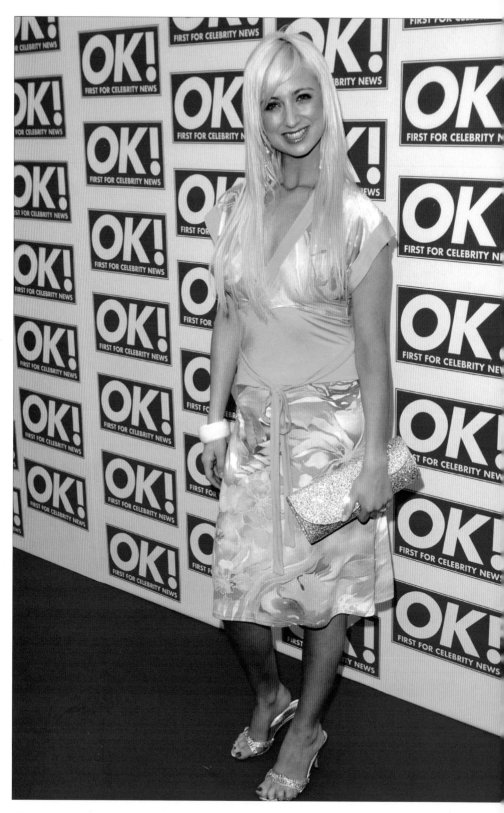

Chantelle's new found fame meant she would soon be invited to plenty of showbiz parties, such as the *OK!* 10th Anniversary bash…

and Hollywood film premieres such as the *Ice Age 2* premiere in London's
icester Square.

Chantelle was determined to use her new-found celebrity to good effect, here promot
anti-bullying campaign Bullywatch London.

which deemed that a person who was famous for having achieved something should win through – but it also looked very much as if he wanted Chantelle to win because he was harbouring increasingly obvious personal feelings for her.

'I hope you win with all my heart,' echoed Pete to Chantelle, with a certain amount of venom in his voice. He had not exactly been encouraging of late. 'Chantelle wants to win, she craves pop stardom with cold-eyed determination, but she should be careful what she wishes for,' he hissed. 'Michael needs to win, he's a performer who needs as much love as possible.'

Barrymore tended to agree. 'I think I should win because I managed to feed this household on a ridiculous budget,' he said.

In their final hours in the house, the celebs started to pack up to leave, with speculation about Chantelle and Preston stronger than ever, not least between the two of them. Neither Chantelle nor Preston knew what was going to happen once they got outside, but she had a typically saucy idea to get him to remember her. 'I've got these knickers,' she told Traci as they packed. 'They're clean and new. I could give them to Preston. He can put them under his pillow.'

By now, *Celebrity Big Brother* had proved so

popular – and this was in part down to Chantelle and Preston – that the producers decided to extend the show's final hours. Initially, it was to have been one programme on the night itself, but this was extended to two. The original format was that the first trio of celebs would be booted out between 8.30pm and 9.30pm, with the last of the three leaving between 10pm and 11pm. 'Originally there was only one show planned, but we have extended it as there are so many housemates left and it's been so popular,' said a *Big Brother* source. 'The winner will be announced about 10.30pm and they will chat to Davina a bit later.'

That final night Traci was first out of the house, drawing cheers as she left. She was 'honoured to be here', she told Davina, even if she had sometimes had 'moments of paranoia'. She had, though, done her bit for the show: she provided glamour and entertainment, even if she was not always the most talkative housemate. And she had increased her profile massively in the UK. Davina made all the right remarks, Traci all the appropriate responses, and with that she was off.

Pete was the next to leave, which meant he'd come in fifth. Dressed for the occasion in a long skirt, he sashayed out of the house to be met with quite a lot of booing. 'Don't touch the make-up!' he screeched to Davina as they sat down. How did he feel about the hostile reception? she wanted to know. 'I'm thrilled by the boos, because it shows I've still got what it takes to make people think about something,' he answered.

He certainly did. Pete had been a revelation: well known among his contemporary musicians, he had nonetheless faded from public view since the glory days of Dead Or Alive. Now he was back with a vengeance: the combination of his extraordinary appearance and that ferocious tongue had made him unmissable viewing. His image was almost the polar opposite of Chantelle's: while she was sweet and innocent, Pete, well, wasn't. But the show's bringing together of the two of them, along with the rest of the household, had had the nation agog.

Davina, certainly, seemed as fascinated as everyone else by Pete, as she continued to grill him in front of the audience. Did he mind not winning? 'I'm thrilled to be here. I was gutted to be in there,' he said.

'Off! Off!' yelled the crowd.

'Don't you wish, bitches,' Pete replied. Would he do it again? 'Not unless they paid me 25 times as much.' What had he learned in the house? 'I learned how to go without sex for three weeks.' How did he feel about the possible re-release of his biggest hit,

'You Spin Me Round', which he had sung in the house? 'Clinically depressed.'

The cameras flicked back to the house, and Chantelle was seen to gasp in shock as it was announced that the next to leave would be Preston. Unlike Pete, he was greeted with rapturous applause and, inevitably, the first thing everyone wanted to know about was the real nature of his relationship with Chantelle. 'She's adorable,' he said. 'She's a little angel.' But they were not a couple, he explained. 'We're just mates. Very, very good mates.' And would they have been a couple if he were single? 'No comment,' said Preston. Camille was waiting for him in the crowd, and that particular remark could not have gone down well with her. And what had he learned? 'I've learned a lot about trust and I'd much rather trust someone and be disappointed than not trust someone,' he replied.

If he was hoping to appease Camille, who must have been spitting tacks by this time, he was certainly choosing an odd way to go about it. 'Of course I fancy Chantelle,' he continued. 'She's got a lovely body. I would be an idiot if I didn't, but I'm afraid I'm already spoken for. The first thing I'm going to say to my girlfriend is tell her I love her and there is nothing I've got to be embarrassed or ashamed of.' Shortly afterwards, he added, 'I love

Camille and I'm going to marry her. I haven't actually proposed, I've only just decided right now.'

As Preston walked off into the night, presumably to start explaining himself to Camille, the cameras swung back to the house. There were only three of them in there now, Chantelle, Michael and Maggot, and tension was really mounting. Could Chantelle conceivably possibly pull it off? Next to go was Maggot, who leaped into the air when his name was announced, only to be informed by Davina that she would come and collect him in half an hour. 'I can't believe it's the two of us,' a slightly dazed Chantelle told Barrymore. He could probably hardly believe it either.

It had been a very eventful three weeks in the house. This had probably been the most talked-about *Big Brother* ever – not surprisingly, really, given the wickedly amusing tasks the housemates had been told to perform and the assiduous attempts of Big Brother to play them off against one another. After all, the programme makers themselves were a good deal more experienced than they had been at the beginning and able to judge just how far to go and what the public would most enjoy or love to hate. And, time after time, they got it right.

And it was partly down to the people within the house. There had been quite a few Chantelle moments when they were all locked in together. Pete, for once, got it wrong when he assumed she was as dumb as she pretended to be. 'Do you know your home address? Are you toilet-trained? Can you cross the road on your own?' he asked.

Chantelle took it all in good humour, but then she could afford to. She'd done spectacularly well. She was also capable of a put-down herself: 'Pete's got an acid tongue,' she said. 'They say you should respect your elders. But, if that's an elder, why should I respect that? I was the youngest, most maturest in there.' The only small moment of conceit came when she was asked about her looks: 'I look like Paris Hilton, not on purpose, but it's just the way it turned out. People are often jealous of my looks, but it's their problem, not mine.'

The minutes ticked on, amid the growing realisation that this was no longer a joke. Chantelle really did look as if she was going to win. Both she and Barrymore could barely take in what was going on around them. He had been tipped as the early winner, but now he was in danger of losing to a girl who had been a complete unknown only three weeks before. After all, he had once been the highest paid and most successful entertainer on British television and there was still a huge amount of affection for him out there, as his reception from the crowd when he had entered the *Big Brother* house had shown. But now a so-called dumb Essex blonde – although she was far more intelligent than people credited her for – looked as if she was about to pip him at the post. 'I don't know what to do,' said Chantelle, hugging him. 'I don't know what to say.'

Barrymore himself, while looking a little stunned, was wise enough not to say anything to show he was as incredulous as he must have felt. And so, as the minutes ticked by, they sat there, the old pro and the blonde pretender, waiting to see which of them would win this year's *Celebrity Big Brother* crown. It was a far cry from when Barrymore had been TV's undisputed king of light entertainment, but then, as he himself was more than aware, the world had changed an awful lot since then.

Finally, the winner was announced – and it was Chantelle, with 56 per cent of the vote against Barrymore's 43.6. The bookies weren't pleased: the odds had shortened on her considerably in the past week or so but, to begin with, at least, she'd been a rank outsider. 'Chantelle is the only one who will cost us money if she wins and she is the shortest-priced favourite we've ever had,' Rupert Adams of William Hill had said. 'She is living the dream of so many people who watch *Big Brother* and her attraction is therefore huge.'

As for everyone else, the final irony of reality TV had come to pass: a complete unknown had won *Celebrity Big Brother* by pretending to be a celebrity herself. Just where could the show go from here?

Barrymore left the house first, to the loudest cheers of the night, and, although he hadn't won, he had clearly redeemed himself in the eyes of at least some of the public. He was quite tearful as he told Davina, 'It's the most brilliant time I've ever had. I'm so excited. What happens from now on is all extras.' He did not mind at all that he had not come first, he said, because 'I've already won because I feel so great. I haven't had the best of times, so just to be asked to take part was brilliant.'

Left alone in the house, the truth began to seep in. A chorus of 'Oh, my Gods' ensued as Chantelle began to realise what was happening to her. She paced up and down the room, still cut off from the outside world in which she was now famous, as she let it all sink in. In the space of three weeks, her world had changed beyond description, from the small scene of her local world in Essex to a stage that was the whole country. Could she believe it? Not quite. 'It shouldn't be me – I'm not a celebrity,' she said afterwards. 'It's quite embarrassing that I've got it.' Embarrassing perhaps, but a triumph, in which a non-celebrity took on the famous and won.

And then, finally, Chantelle herself appeared. Dressed in a white minidress, she emerged to raucous cheering and realised, perhaps for the first time, that she really was now a genuine celeb. Her mother was in the crowd and was as wildly buoyed up as anyone. 'I can't feel anything except happiness and excitement,' she said.

Looking rather dazed – 'I'm just, like, wowsers' – Chantelle settled down for a chat with the presenter. 'Davina? Are you sure you've got this right?' she asked. 'You are joking, aren't you?'

Davina was not joking and Chantelle was now informed that she was to be awarded £25,000 for winning the show. What would she do with the money? 'I would like to take my mum and everyone on holiday, because that would be a nice thing to do,' she said. 'Once that's out of the way – I don't know. Go shopping. Make-up, clothes, orange lipstick – I need one of them. I've got to make sure I get a stock of that. That's a lot of money, a hell of a lot of money. I really don't know what I'll do. I will be able to pay the debts I owe my mum.'

And what, she was asked, were her thoughts about Preston? 'When people keep going on about, "Do you fancy him, do you fancy him?" you begin to think about it,' she said. 'At one point I thought, I really like this boy, and I realised I trusted him. I would marry him, but I don't want to get married for a very, very long time.'

Of course, all that did was to add more fuel to the flames, but Chantelle was at least being honest. Clearly, there would have to be some heavy-duty talks all round after the cameras were finally switched off.

Meanwhile, she was being a little disingenuous, insisting, 'I don't fancy him. I know I liked him a little bit more on the Saturday afternoon when George was found cheating again. It was because I trusted him and to be able to trust someone in there is a really, really big thing. [But] I ain't copped off with him, honest. There weren't no friendly contact between us.'

But the atmosphere in the house had been almost bound to draw them together, as she herself acknowledged. 'We're two young people, we like the same things and we trusted each other,' she said. 'Those things bring you together in an environment like that. At one point I thought, I really like this boy. Then I liked him a bit more than that. I didn't go into the house looking for love – and I came out of the house without love. I'm going to enjoy being one of Britain's most eligible bachelorettes. And I'm open to offers.'

What about the other celebs? Davina asked. Were

they annoyed that what Elizabeth Hurley refers to as 'a civilian' was in their midst? 'I didn't get the feeling they resented me, but I felt maybe I made some people feel stupid,' she confessed. 'If I did get into an argument, some people might have said, "You're not a celeb." I didn't want that. But I knew when to stand up for myself – when it got a bit too much.'

And what was she going to do now she really was a celebrity? 'Mum, what am I going to do next?' she called out.

'Live the dream!' yelled Vivien.

'I'm living it!' cried Chantelle. But she was not going to change, she said. 'I'm just little old me.'

As for why she had won, 'I think it's just because I'm down-to-earth and easygoing,' she said.

She was certainly right there. Compared with some of the real celebs she'd spent the last three weeks with, Chantelle was a picture of normality. And, on top of that, she had accomplished a peculiarly modern dream. With no particular talents to speak of, she'd been on television and had achieved that all-important goal of our times – to become famous. And the best was yet to come.

7

There Were Three of Us in The Relationship...

Now that Chantelle and Preston were back in the real world, there were quite a few issues to be resolved, and fast. The most pressing one was: were they going to be together after all? And what about Camille? It was a bit of a mess, and Preston, caught in the middle of it, didn't seem to know what to do. Obviously, he owed it to Camille to behave as well as possible, but then didn't he owe something to Chantelle? It was all very difficult and, to begin with, he was torn.

'I'm sorry but I told a lie... I love Chantelle,' he declared a couple of days after coming out of the house. 'I love Camille and I want to do right by her. But now I also love Chantelle, and she's going to be in my life. It's messy, but the truth is I love them both. I fancied Chantelle straight away – who wouldn't? She's gorgeous, brilliant, funny, everything I look for in a girl. I'm not bothered whether she has blonde hair or fake nails. That's not why I like her. I like her because she's the way she is. That's why she's sexy.'

Almost immediately, it became clear that the bond between the two of them was even stronger than it had appeared while they were on screen. Simply because of the rather unusual way in which they met, it had been all too easy to dismiss the relationship as a publicity stunt or, at the very least, as happening because they were both in an artificial and pressured setting where emotions were prone to get out of hand. But now, away from all the hype, it looked like the real thing.

'We had an almost instant connection of the kind I never thought I'd experience. She's like a soulmate,' said Preston, and, if he thought his relationship with Camille could continue after this, he was a truly optimistic man. 'She was like my girlfriend in the house – but now we're back in the real world. I told a white lie to Davina because I was in a state of shock coming out of the house. I realised there'd be a lot of speculation and didn't want to hurt anyone. So, when she asked what had gone on, I just said we were friends.'

Preston admitted that he had not thought a great deal about Camille when he was in the house, but in a way that should have been no surprise. The programme makers purposely cut the contestants off from the outside world and put them into an unreal atmosphere when anything beyond must scarcely seem to exist. 'Life in the house was like a perfect bubble and Chantelle was my playmate, it was like, "What shall we do today?"' said Preston. 'She kept me sane. We forgot about the cameras and just had a laugh and a flirt. I was naive and stupid because I didn't realise how it was going to look to those on the outside. We never thought about life beyond the house. I stupidly thought everyone would think, It's so great they've made such good friends. When I had my arm around her or held her hand, I thought nothing of it. It was a natural thing to do. It was dumb of me to think Camille wouldn't be hurt by some of the things we got up to.'

Yet he still seemed not to realise that their relationship was at an end. It would have been intolerable for Camille – and Chantelle likewise – to continue with things the way they were now, but Preston still rather unrealistically expressed the hope that the two women, who had been introduced at the after-show party, would be able to get on. But could they be friends?

The answer was no, though Preston did try. 'I said to Camille, "Do you want to meet Chantelle?"' he related. 'She said, "OK," and I led her across the room. They said, "Hi," to each other. It was a bit awkward to say the least. I want them to be friends – I love both of them. I think it went OK. But who knows? Time will tell.'

To be fair to him, towards the end of their time in the house, Preston himself had begun to realise that his girlfriend might be a bit put out. 'I got a bit stressed about it, and told Chantelle, "We have to go back to the real world,"' he recalled. 'I knew the bubble was going to burst and everyone was going to start to intrude.'

Poor old Preston. He was clearly trying to make the best of it, but every time he opened his mouth it was almost bound to enrage Camille more. 'Camille and Chantelle do have a lot in common,' he insisted. 'They have the same aura, it's really subtle. I liked Chantelle because I saw a lot of my girlfriend in her, and my sister and my mum. They're alike and I just want to look after them all. It doesn't matter to me whether a woman is blonde or brunette. I just like girls you can trust and someone who trusts you. She needs to be someone who is fun to be around, someone you respect. But she does have to be nice-looking. Camille was giving me a few evils when I came out. After the camera stopped, I took her aside and told her she'd nothing to worry about. She said, "Fine." We haven't had a proper chat but we will have to talk.'

They most certainly would. Preston kept digging himself deeper with everything he said, as when he speculated on what would happen with Chantelle if he was single. 'If I was single, who knows what would happen? She's a brilliant mate, and I could never be bored with her, and that's what you look for in a wife. Her parents split up and so did mine, so we've been through the same stuff.' Or, to put it another way, he was besotted with her, they had a huge amount in common and she had all the qualities he would look for in a wife. Preston might not have realised that he was about to split from Camille, but he wasn't leaving the rest of the world in much doubt. Quite apart from anything else, he had, literally, hardly seen her. He had been doing a whirlwind of the television studios, appearing on *CD:UK* and *Top Of The Pops*, among a good deal else, and simply had not had time to talk it over with her.

Chantelle herself also appeared to be in a slight state of denial about what was happening, although she was quite open about how she felt to be introduced to Camille. 'It was the awkwardest moment I have ever had in my life. I walked into the room at the party and Preston said, "Come and meet my girlfriend." She and I looked at each other and said, "Hi." It was pretty awkward. Preston said, "Well done, I'm really pleased for you," and then, the next time I saw him and Camille, we all said goodbye. Now there is nothing to be awkward about. I want her to see it that I kept him sane in there. I hope she knows that because, if he had broken down crying, it would have been awful.'

Of course, others had witnessed that awkward moment, and it was a bit sticky. 'She [Camille] turned around and wrapped her arms around him, but he didn't respond,' said one of the fellow guests. 'Camille's big smile turned into a frown.' And then Chantelle arrived. 'He [Preston] pushed past everyone to give her a huge hug. He grabbed her, they kissed. When he realised everyone was staring at them, he dashed off to get Camille and introduced them. It was awkward.' That was putting it mildly. Clearly, something would have to give.

Chantelle's mother, however, played down any tensions. 'I think they got on really well,' said Vivien. 'They had been shown a few clips on the screen of my daughter and Preston getting friendly so I don't know how that made Camille feel but, like Chantelle said, there is nothing going on. They are just really good friends and at the end of the day he's got a girlfriend.'

Camille, unsurprisingly, took a different view. Talking to another *Big Brother* contestant, Craig Coates, at the after-show party, she appeared far from happy with what had been going on. 'He wouldn't normally look twice at someone like her – he doesn't usually go for blonde slappers,' she said in a tone that made her real feelings totally clear. 'Chantelle's not stupid, though – she was playing the game and she lured him in. I knew he didn't like her – it was all her. And it was edited to make it look like more than it was. Chantelle was leading him on. I could tell he wasn't really interested in her.

'She's such a hypocrite. One week, she was saying she would never look at another woman's man and yet she was still trying it on with him and desperately trying to get him. She just wanted the attention and publicity. She was leading him on – anyone could see that she was interested in him. I think *Big Brother* wanted her to win from the beginning and made it look worse than it was. The show's bosses knew that a romance would make good viewing and they wanted them to get together. I feel like the producers wanted to split me and Preston up and for him and Chantelle to be together because that way *Big*

Brother will make more money. If Preston and Chantelle were a couple they would make loads from magazine deals. That would all be publicity for *Big Brother*.'

But Chantelle didn't appear unduly concerned. In fact, she could hardly contain herself when she started to talk about her new friend. 'He is so cute, I just wanted to squeeze his cheeks,' she said. 'He's a lovely bloke and really genuine. Once Jodie left, it was just us two. If he was in the bedroom, I was in the bedroom. If he was in the living room, I was in the living room. It just happened that way. We didn't set out to do it. We like each other, so it is inevitable. To be in a close environment like that and to feel that way is the nicest thing.'

But, like Preston, she said she was aware there might be repercussions outside the house and that there were also good reasons not to be too close to him initially. 'In the first week particularly, I found it easier to be around Jodie,' she said. 'I avoided Preston and Maggot like the plague because of the task. I didn't want them to suspect I was a fake. Once Jodie was gone, my friendship with Preston grew.'

And she played down that infamous in-house marriage proposal. 'It was lovely when he said that, really nice,' she said. 'Any girl who has that said to her is going to be happy.' But, again like Preston,

Chantelle soon decided it might be a good idea to cool off. 'I calmed it down a bit,' she said. 'We never did anything wrong. We didn't snog or do anything that could be classed as cheating.'

Not that Preston was the sort of man Chantelle usually went for. 'I like them a bit muscular – stocky blokes,' she said. 'But he's a really wonderful bloke. I wouldn't change anything about him. We will definitely see each other again as friends. I want to say thank you to him for how he made it for me, as much as I did for him. Thanks for being you.'

Understandably, everyone was very keen to know what Chantelle had really thought of her other housemates as well, and she was only too happy to oblige. Of Jodie she said, 'She got misunderstood by everyone and she was only one of three stars in there I actually recognised. Good luck to her. I didn't have a good or bad view on her.'

She also liked Faria. 'She is a nice kind person. I did ask her about Sven and she told me all about what went on. I don't think she wanted to go into detail because she had come on the show to show everyone what she is really like.'

Rula, however, had not gone down so well. 'She was playing a game. She hugged everyone and ruffled their hair and touched their shoulders. She was bossy. I think George was right when he said she was out to win. Rula's a female version of George. If they were ten years younger, they'd get together – and that would be an awful thought.'

On the subject of George himself, though, Chantelle was cutting. 'He would look at me like I was some stupid little girl. But once he was up for nomination he turned into this nice sweet bloke. This man claims he is after the youth vote but I would never have voted for him. I think George looked down on me, like I was a scatty girl who was uneducated. He said he couldn't believe that I lived in Essex and am a vegetarian because most of them come from north London. What does it matter where you're from?'

She was also rather cautious about Dennis. 'When he said he wanted to have sex with me, it worried me,' she said. 'The idea makes me ill. Especially since I had to sleep in the bed next to him. I felt I had a pair of beady eyes on me all the time and asked him to stop it. He became a snake in the grass.'

Traci she couldn't really fathom. 'I don't think she wanted to talk about her life. I don't know anything about her. One time, Pete said to her, if you love my shoes, then get down and lick them. And do you know what? She actually was about to get down and lick them. Amazing.'

Chantelle was a bit hurt when it came to Pete. 'I

thought he was all right but since I've come out people have told me what he was really saying about me. It upsets me. He has an acid tongue and can be wicked.'

But she did like Maggot. 'He turned out to be just the nicest bloke ever. The agitation caused him to have a rash. Poor man. He and Traci were a bit flirty, but I didn't think anything would happen.'

As for Barrymore, 'I was worried I might say the wrong thing and he might flare up,' she said. 'We were friends in the house but I don't think we will meet up for a drink – well, certainly not an alcoholic one. I can't believe I asked him if he wanted a light ale in the house. He is a funny man and entertained us.'

The future looked rosy, but not just for Chantelle. Many of the housemates were benefiting from their stay in the house: Pete had apparently been offered a chat show, there was talk of Barrymore making a comeback on British television and Preston's band, the Ordinary Boys, had a single in the Top Ten and a forthcoming tour that was sold out. The only person who appeared to have done badly out of it was George, as even he was now beginning to realise.

Of course, there was also Jodie. She had not held

back in her opinions of the housemates since leaving, and she was not prepared to do so now. But in the end it had worked out for her: she had had a great many job offers and her career appeared still to be on track.

There were to be no peace talks with the others, though. And, when Jodie attended the after-show party, it was under duress. 'Apparently, I am contracted to go to the last eviction winner's night,' she said. 'I have tried desperately to get out of it but it's a no-win situation. If I don't go, then I won't get paid for the whole thing and I am not going to allow that to happen. Apart from meeting Chantelle, the only good thing about doing *BB* was the amount I was getting paid. As if I'm gonna go through that whole vile public shredding for free!'

Nor had she even begun to forgive Barrymore for what happened between them in the house. 'Bullymore [sic] is vile in my opinion,' she said in a notice posted on her website. Stuart Lubbock's family do not know how he died. I hope that Bullymore doesn't earn a shred of respect while inside the *Big Brother* house.'

Given that level of feeling, it was hardly surprising that she was in no mood to mend bridges when she was at the party itself. Barrymore did actually try to make up, but Jodie was having none of it. 'He was trying to kiss me,' she said afterwards. 'He came over and said, "Oh, come on, one last kiss," and I was like, "No!"'

Apart from Jodie and George – although even Jodie did well out of it – the show was judged to have been an enormous success. But most of all, of course, that applied to Chantelle. 'It was a very clever joke by the production team,' said Peter Bazalgette, chairman of Endemol, which made the programme. 'Nobody thought for a moment she'd end up winning. It's hilarious. It's very Channel 4 – that's where you'd expect to find this kind of slightly postmodern convoluted joke.'

It wasn't a joke for everyone, though. It did seem as if Barrymore really might be able to make a comeback after this – something that would have been inconceivable even a couple of years earlier. 'If offers come in, I'd be delighted to take them if they are the right things to do,' he said. 'It's not down to me. It's up to those that make offers but if something comes along, then I'd love to work here again.'

The experience in the show had changed him in other ways, too. For years, his partner had been Shaun Davis, and Barrymore revealed they were to get hitched. 'We are planning to get married. And I can't wait. I love Shaun and want to spend the rest of my life with him. He's my rock. They've just changed the law in New Zealand, too. Marriage is on the cards. It's a high possibility. No woman or man is an island. I learned in the house how much we do need each other.'

Shaun himself had been watching the proceedings with some anxiety. 'Michael was excited but also very nervous,' he said. 'He hadn't been on the screen in the UK for five years. We were all very apprehensive as to what the crowd's response might be but the support was almost too much for him to take in. When Michael started crying, I felt very emotional for him. It was a delayed reaction to the crowd's overwhelming response and the build-up to the whole show.'

Barrymore might have been a draw for the crowds, but even he couldn't match Pete Burns when it came to the downright bizarre. Pete, like the rest of them, was happy to chat about his time in the household, but was happier still when it came to talking about himself – or, specifically, the amount of plastic surgery he'd had. His was such an extraordinary appearance that people were fascinated by what he'd had done. And, judging from what he said after leaving the house, it was an extremely painful experience.

'I prayed for death,' he explained. 'The pain was so

intense I was crawling on the floor screaming. When I was undergoing corrective surgery to try to put things right, my condition was so severe that before every operation I had to sign a consent form accepting that they might have to amputate my face – so I never knew if I was going to wake up with any features left. And people ask me if it was a nightmare in the *Big Brother* house!

'After what I've been through, a little hardship for a reality-TV show was nothing. I only did *Celebrity Big Brother* to raise some money. I also hope that what happened to me might help people realise that those extreme make-over shows don't tell the story of how painful plastic surgery can be. I'm totally happy to talk about the other housemates, even the dreadful Jodie Marsh and that vile individual Chantelle. But I don't give a damn about them – or that pipsqueak squirt Preston. All that programme was for me was a very highly paid gig. I fulfilled my contract. And, in case anyone's wondering, I was paid an awful lot more than £50,000.'

The surgical work began in the 1980s, shortly after Pete became a big star. 'I had a nose job four times – each one a disaster,' he said. 'Then in 1987 I had cheek implants. They were a complete disaster, too – so they had to take them out and insert another pair.

They were also a disaster, so they had to take them out as well. In 1989, I had probably the first Botox in this country. Then I started lip augmentation. I've never had anything done to my eyes. Nor have I had a brow lift. But last September I had to have most of my face removed from its structure – all this stuff scraped out – and then sewn back on.'

Poor old Pete was suffering from all the chemicals he'd had injected into his lips over the years. 'It started after I had a piece of tissue inserted into my upper lip. At first, it was fine, but then about six years ago I went to another doctor and asked him to remove it. But he said he didn't need to, and instead injected this stuff all around the tissue and at first it looked great. He had to keep doing repeats. The doctor was using all sorts of different products and my lips were getting bigger and smaller on a daily basis. Then one day I was due to do a show with the Scissor Sisters and I was in severe pain. The doctor said the top lip was too heavy and needed lifting. When he stitched me up it never healed. All these procedures cost me in excess of £36,000.

'The doctor more or less closed the door on me. So I consulted many other specialists. But the consensus was that various parts of my face would have to be amputated. I only had to turn my head by a fraction of an inch and my skin would split and this horrible gunk would come spurting out of my cheeks. It would fly two or three feet. Loads of it. It was really disgusting. I'm not the suicidal type, but in those dark days I'd take 20 or 30 sleeping pills in a day and hope I didn't come round. I was on intravenous morphine and pethidine – but the pain was unbelievably intense.'

It was one of his fans who put him on to a surgeon who could clean up the mess. 'The surgeon said he could get the gunk out,' said Pete. 'But it would take four months. When he opened me up, it was worse than he thought and it took more than 17 months. I have had more than a hundred reconstructive operations. And I still have to go back. I haven't counted up how much it has all cost me. But I know this much – it's certainly more than £100,000.'

Yet Pete was adamant that he didn't do any of this to make himself look like a woman – he just wanted to look like himself. 'None of this is about wanting to look like a woman. I don't want to be a woman – I'm proud of my manhood and I was very happily married for 25 years in a normal heterosexual relationship. No, for me the surgery was never vanity – it was a matter of sanity. I never recognised my face as a child; I didn't think it was the face I should have been born with. I never used to wear much make-up. But I have to now because of the scars and stitch marks left by all the corrective surgery.'

Pete had been married to Lynne, but they had separated and he was now with Michael Simpson. 'I don't see gender,' he said. 'When I walk into a room I see people, and I can easily be attracted to either men or women. I met Lynne and she was someone I loved. Way down the line, I met Michael – and he's someone I love. Lynne and I still love each other, but not in the way we did. We're all the best of friends.'

Michael Simpson had unwittingly been the cause of one of the memorable moments on the show. It was he who, three years previously, had given Pete the notorious fur coat that led the police to take action against him. 'Michael bought it for me in 2003,' said Pete. 'It is actually made from the fur of Colobus monkeys – which are used in vivisection and totally legal when it comes to fur coats. I demanded the police gave it straight back to me. What an absurd waste of taxpayers' money.'

As for his behaviour to the women in the house: 'I'm used to people accusing me of not liking girls,' Pete said. 'I do a great job of being a girl, I know all their tricks and I understand their artillery, why would I want to be one? Those arguments with the girls in the house, they generated hostility against me. And without exception most of the hostility I have ever encountered has come from females. The way I am just seems to throw them. George Galloway told me that all the girls in the house started wearing more make-up and sexier clothes as a reaction to me. When I was trying to get one of my nose jobs, a psychiatrist told me he thought I'd be happier with a vagina. What rubbish. I really like having a dick.'

Like Rula, Pete appeared on the show out of necessity. 'I did *Big Brother* for the money,' he said. 'Everything I do is financially motivated now because I'm nearly 47 and I can't go back to a normal life. I can hardly get a job in Sainsbury's. During my cosmetic journey, I had to sell my house and a lot of my publishing rights – even to "You Spin Me Round". I could have gone broke and sat around feeling sorry for myself – or get off my arse and fight back. I'm glad I chose to do that. And that's why, even though I didn't particularly enjoy it, I have no regrets about *Celebrity Big Brother*.'

Two reasons for *Celebrity Big Brother*'s enormous success, in Peter Bazalgette's eyes, lay in its casting and the tasks. And an enormous amount of work had gone on behind the scenes before the makers were able to pull it together. The initial shortlist had included 500 people before it was whittled down to 40 and the serious task of persuading the celebs to sign up began. 'We have to get people to trust us, and to see if we think they are good and they like us,' said Peter Gair, the show's producer. 'We are brutally honest with them. We call it "the talk of doom", telling them about the intense media interest they will face.'

The planning of the show had been both imaginative and extremely thorough, so that it yielded countless memorable moments. 'Because it's for Channel 4 and it's *Big Brother* we can take a few more risks and be slightly left-field,' said Gair. 'It's an organic process. You can't just tick a few boxes – tabloid favourite, ageing pop star, member of girl band, an eccentric. If you try and do that, it won't work. You have to think of how these people will work together in a confined area. It's all about their relationship with each other.' And, of course, for one of them, fame.

Justly, the placing of Chantelle into the household was being hailed as the biggest success of all the various aspects of the show. 'The invention of Chantelle was a superb piece of casting,' said the social commentator Peter York. '*Celebrity Big Brother* is a work of genius, not least in the way the cast of characters are put together. The programme is being made by people with a big cultural imagination and a long memory to think of people like Pete Burns and George Galloway. Even the acts of casual cruelty they inflicted on the contestants were inspired.'

8

How it All Began

And then there was the winner. Chantelle herself had not had the slightest idea she would win. 'What you see is what you get with Chantelle,' said her mother. 'She's just like she is on television. She's down-to-earth, totally natural. She had no idea she'd get all this attention. She was working part-time on a make-up counter in a store in the West End before going into the house and she thought she'd be going back there this week. She asked me to keep any clippings from the papers if there was any mention of her because she thought there might be a few. The pile is two feet high.' Vivien was spilling over with pride for her daughter.

Some details about Chantelle's background had already begun to emerge, and now more was coming to light. She had been educated at Bromsford School in Wickford, near Basildon, and had left school at 16 to work in an office and then a bank. And it was then that she began to realise she wanted a more interesting life. 'After a while, she told me, "I can't do a nine-to-five office job,"' Vivien recalled. 'She wanted to be a top model. She's always been a girlie girl and loved clothes and make-up. When we go to Lakeside shopping centre, boys and girls shout out. She just puts her head down. She gets sideways glances all the time when we're out. She doesn't know they're looking at her, but I'm looking at them looking at her.'

'Chantelle did so well because she was just herself,' said Jo Carnegie, deputy editor of *Heat* magazine. 'She was good value: funny, good-natured and not afraid to get stuck in or laugh at herself. Girls like her because she has the same worries about her weight and love life et cetera as the rest of them; guys like her because she is fun, curvy and nice to look at. There are millions of girls like her, only she is the one who embarked on the dream. People are engrossed by her.'

As for Chantelle herself, she still could not quite believe what was happening. The day after her win, she stepped into her new life proper, giving an interview with Dermot O'Leary about the whole experience and what she was going to do now. She couldn't stop smiling and said she was running on adrenaline, although she admitted that at first she had thought the result was not actually true. 'I was like, Hang on a minute, and then I started thinking this was a joke, another cruel task,' she said. 'I didn't know what to think, being in that house on my own.'

Of course, everyone was still fascinated to know how she had actually pulled it off. She had been in a house full of seasoned performers, after all, and yet she had managed to convince the lot of them that she was something other than the person she was. How on earth had she managed that? Faria, Michael, Dennis and Traci had been the easiest to fool, she said, because they had been living abroad. 'They had been out of the country and so didn't know so much about what was going on in this country.' As for the others – well, she just avoided them as much as she could.

As for the future, Chantelle seemed as nonplussed as everyone else did. 'I am waiting for tomorrow and when tomorrow comes I am going to wait for the next day and see what comes,' she said. 'It hasn't sunk in yet. I feel I am in a dream, watching some else's life at the moment.'

She needed the services of a professional to look after her, though, and fast. Everyone, including the man himself, had been happily assuming that it would be Max Clifford who would look after her interests, but, rather to everyone's surprise, Chantelle decided to go with his rival John Noel instead. There was no problem about doing this: no contracts had been signed and Chantelle herself had never actually agreed to work with Clifford. 'Max has every right to be upset: he didn't even get the courtesy of an apology,' said a friend. 'He's actually philosophical about it, though. Since he never signs a contract with any clients, he accepts that these things will sometimes happen.'

Actually, Chantelle's decision made sense. Clifford was known for helping people to cash in on their newfound fame very quickly, whereas John Noel had helped people build long-term careers. He was Davina McCall's agent, as well as representing the most successful *Big Brother* contestant to date, Jade Goody. And so it was quite understandable that Chantelle felt he was the right person to look after her interests. She was canny enough to realise that the interest in her could evaporate quite as quickly as it had appeared, and obviously she wanted to build something more solid while the fascination in her was still there. Nonetheless, no one involved wanted to make an enemy of Clifford. 'If Max wants to get on the phone and talk about it, then we can,' said an understandably anxious John Noel.

Already offers were flooding in, among them that proposal to record 'I Want It Right Now' with Kandyfloss. Chantelle was so far committing herself to nothing. 'It's still very early days,' said a spokeswoman. 'Chantelle hasn't had a chance to go through all the offers coming in, so we won't be making any firm plans until next week.'

Some people, though, were acting fast. A sound engineer on *Big Brother* found one of Chantelle's lipsticks in the house and put it up for sale on eBay. 'I thought a fan would like it in their personal collection. It's the real thing,' he explained.

And, early days or not, one other fact had emerged about Chantelle Houghton, the Paris Hilton lookalike. The agency Fake Faces was looking for a new doppelganger – for Chantelle – and Jacqueline Blair, a 19-year-old call-centre worker from Mid Calder, West Lothian, fitted the bill. 'I am over the moon she won, because it means a career for me, too,' said Jacqueline. 'I have had lots of invitations to appear on daytime TV shows.' A lookalike for a lookalike? Could postmodern television get more ironic than this?

Chantelle was now recognised all over the

country, and had her own agent, offers galore and a very bright future ahead. Scarcely able to believe her good luck, she was beginning to reveal exactly how she had ended up as the only non-celeb in a celebrity household – and how she had got to where she was now.

It seemed a couple of models, and her admiration for them, was what propelled Chantelle to try to make a name for herself. The first of these was Jordan, Jodie's great rival, who had provided a great deal of inspiration for our heroine. 'I had always dreamed of being a model and that's why I followed Jordan's career,' said Chantelle. 'I love her and love what she's done in her life. I hope I can achieve the same. She came from nowhere, just like me. Jordan hasn't had it easy. She hasn't had things handed on a plate, she's worked hard for it. She has survived all the knocks. It's fantastic what she has achieved, especially since she's now a mum with two kids. She's worked hard to get somewhere – and I will, too.'

Funnily enough, Chantelle had met Jordan, although the two had not got to know each other. It had been a couple of years previously, when Chantelle entered a *Max Power* Babe contest. 'Jordan was a judge and she came over and wished us all well,' she recalled. 'But I didn't do very well in the contest, so I never got the chance to meet her again. I don't know if she watched *Big Brother* but it would be nice to talk with her and maybe get some advice and tips.'

She was being a little overoptimistic there. Jordan did indeed keep an eye on anyone she thought might be a rival and, in the weeks after Chantelle had emerged from the house, especially when she and Preston formally became a couple, it emerged that Jordan thought she might be a real threat. This manifested itself in vague and ominous mutterings about the new kid on the block, but more of that later.

Chantelle's earlier years fascinated many: how she got her first break at the age of 18, when she entered a *Motorcycle Monthly* Babe competition and was signed up as an official Motorcycle Babe, before appearing as a Page 3 girl – although a repeat of that was ruled out now that she was famous. 'It was like a dream come true, an amazing opportunity,' she said. 'I went on tour around the country and used to visit bike races. It was such fun. I met loads of people and it really kick-started my modelling career. Then things really started to get busy for me.'

It was when people began to notice her resemblance to Paris Hilton that her career really took off. 'On one of the first proper shoots I did, the photographer told me. "You are just like Paris." It got me thinking, so I emailed some photos of myself to an agency. I got a call within seconds and they didn't actually believe I was for real! They thought I'd copied pictures of Paris and sent them in trying to fool them!'

Her more recent role model was none other than Caprice. The blonde model had been on the previous series of *Celebrity Big Brother* and it was this that set Chantelle thinking that perhaps she should have a go at getting on such a programme. Of course, she was not initially thinking of *Celebrity Big Brother*, but, as things stood, she had probably ended up doing much better than she would have done in the 'civilian' version.

'I loved the show and loved seeing Caprice in it – I watched it loads,' she said, as she began to explain for the first time how it all had come about. 'I kept thinking, I wonder if I could do that. At the end of the series, an advert came up saying they were looking for people for the new series of *Big Brother*. And I just thought I should give it a go. I went to the auditions and the producers asked, "Why do you want to be on *Big Brother*?" I told them, "I don't know." Everyone else was running around shouting and screaming and taking off their clothes and I just sat there saying I didn't know. And the truth is, I still don't know why I applied. But I'm glad I did.'

Of course, initially she didn't actually make it into the *Big Brother* house, although she did meet a few of the people who had made the grade. 'I met Science and Mary the witch,' she said. 'So it was weird when I switched on to see the show and they were there. That could have been me, I was thinking.'

And that, it appeared, had been that. Chantelle didn't give it much more thought, other than to muse on the fickle nature of television, until the following December, when, out of the blue, the producers of *Celebrity Big Brother* rang. It suddenly became clear that, far from her dreams of television stardom being over, she was on the verge of being offered a much bigger deal. 'It was weird that they called me back,' she said in something of an understatement. 'I must have made an impression. They said I'd be one of six ordinary people being put into the house with six celebs.'

And that is what she had been expecting, but the producers of the show had been playing games with everyone from the start. She was soon to discover that she was not going on the show on the basis that had been outlined: instead, she would be the one non-celebrity in a house full of famous people. And, of course, before that she would have to keep it all completely to herself. 'I thought something wasn't right but I just went along with it. I was sworn to secrecy. I couldn't tell a soul – not even my mum. I could only let them know the night before I went into the house. It was terrible having to keep it all a secret. I was reading in the papers that Michael Barrymore and Pete Burns and Faria Alam were going in the house. Most people would be nervous about that but for some reason I wasn't.'

And now, for the moment at least, she was one of their number. The perks of celebrity were also beginning to come her way, something she found extraordinary. One example was Take That's upcoming tour. Chantelle had been a great fan of the band as a teenager, her particular favourite being another *Celebrity Big Brother* winner, Mark Owen, but she had assumed she would not be able to get tickets for their tour. It seems she was wrong.

She would have loved to see them in concert but all the tickets were sold out, she said. But then, 'Someone said to me, "Well, now you're a celebrity you will get a ticket." And I just said, "I'm not a celebrity – what are you talking about?" But this is what people are telling me. I still can't believe it. I don't feel like a celebrity. To me, I'm just Chantelle – I'm just the same person I was three weeks ago.'

Something she was keen to set straight, though,

was the matter of her intelligence. She was keen to make the point that she was no dumb blonde. 'In the house, people like George and Dennis thought I was stupid,' she said. 'But I'm not. I don't mind when people take the mickey. I am a fun person. But I will stand up for myself and show people I'm not a dumb blonde.' Of course she wasn't. She had just hoodwinked a whole bunch of celebrities, some of them household names, into thinking she was who she said she was and not who she really was. It took some sharp manoeuvring to do that.

Of course, people were not only fascinated about where Chantelle had come from, but about where she was going, not least with Preston. With every minute that passed, speculation intensified as to what would happen next. Preston had now publicly declared his love for her and Chantelle repaid the compliment. 'I feel love for him. It's not lust. It's love,' she said. She was becoming decidedly more forthcoming about the person who was shortly to become her new beau. Preston, she said, was the very first person who had ever chatted her up. He had looked after her in a caring, devoted way, she added. As for that 'I love Chantelle… I fancied her straight away' remark, she was thrilled. 'I am really flattered that Preston said that about me. I really want us to stay in touch. The moment I saw him on that first night, I thought he would be the show pin-up. He isn't the typical guy I go for, because I like men with a bit of meat on them. But I do like tall men. We grew a lot closer once I had passed my secret mission about pretending to be a pop star and I could relax a lot more. When he cuddled and hugged me, it really made me feel better. He is so nice to be around.'

Chantelle was obviously as besotted with Preston as he was with her. 'Nothing was too much trouble,' she went on. 'He even went into the Diary Room on my behalf and asked for foundation. Bless him! He's the kindest boy I've known. It's funny, because men never chat me up when I am out. They look, but they never come over. So it was flattering to have all this attention from Preston. We would be together all the time. It wasn't planned, it just happened that way.'

Actually, according to Chantelle, both were a bit concerned about matters getting out of hand. 'Everyone kept teasing us about our friendship and it got to that point where I started thinking, Do I fancy Preston? And then I realised that the reason I liked him so much was because I trusted him. There was a point one night when Preston was saying all these lovely things to me. He even said he'd marry me if he was single. It was a surprise. One time he said to me, "If I do anything or say anything, then throw a glass of water in my face to cool me down!" It was after that talk that we tried to keep our distance. I tried to cool it for his benefit. The others were winding us up and I knew he started to think about how our relationship might look to his girlfriend.'

She was also worried about how it would make her look to the viewers. She didn't, after all, want to be labelled as the sort of woman who went around stealing other people's boyfriends. 'I was worried what girls outside might think,' she said. 'I knew they'd be watching, all these girls with posters of him on the wall. I was thinking, They will think Preston's lovely and there is this blonde taking him away from his girlfriend. I was so worried about all this, which is why we calmed it down. [But] Preston and I will stay friends. If we hadn't been in the house, we wouldn't have had the chance to be alone together and get close.'

Asked about her response to Camille calling her a 'blonde slapper', Chantelle sensibly refused to get drawn into it. She was content to say, 'Preston and I are soulmates who helped each other survive the house. It's been the most amazing experience of my life and I wouldn't change a thing.'

William Hill, as ever, was watching the progress of the two with a sharp eye. It had been offering 8/1 on the two of them getting engaged: now it closed the book. 'If Preston pops the question, he will not be the only one on his knees,' said a jovial Rupert Adams. 'But we are still offering odds of 12/1 on the two of them actually tying the knot in 2006.'

Another bookie popped up at this point, wondering whether there might have been some nefarious goings-on behind the scenes at the show. It concerned Barrymore, who had been on long odds until the very last day of the run, until suddenly a lot more people seemed to be backing him to win. 'Originally, we had Barrymore as the 3/1 favourite but he soon fell out of favour with the public after his rows with Jodie Marsh,' said spokesman David Williams. 'Eventually, he went out to a 16/1 outsider and stayed in double-figure odds right up until the final day. But on Friday some strange things seemed to start to happen and everyone began backing him, bringing his price down to 8/1. With such a firm favourite in Chantelle, the overall result hardly seemed in doubt. But it was surprising that Barrymore beat both Preston and Maggot.'

Channel 4 denied point-blank that anything funny had gone on. 'The fact is that Michael grew in popularity,' said a spokeswoman. 'Of course there was no skulduggery. If you look at the reception Michael got when he arrived and when he left, it just shows that he still has a strong following which was also reflected in the end vote. Once someone was voted off, the whole process just started again.'

The public was not bothered: they'd got the winner they wanted. Chantelle's father was another family member who was overjoyed. 'I'm so proud of my Chantelle,' Alan said. 'I've only been able to chat to her briefly as she's been rushed off her feet since winning. She was over the moon and I don't think any of us expected the public to take her to their hearts like that. All her friends and family can't wait for her to come home so we can tell her how special she is. Her friends are desperate for us to throw a party. It's going to be no expense spared. It's not every day that your daughter becomes a star.'

And more people continued to turn up from Chantelle's past. One of these was 22-year-old Carly Wainwright, a very old friend who released a set of pictures of the 15-year-old Chantelle sporting brunette hair, taken when the two were at Bromsford School in Wickford. 'She always wanted to be famous,' said Carly. 'Ever since I've known her, she's wanted something different. She always had a dream and I guess she's living it now. I'm so happy for her.

'She always had long hair and was always playing with it,' said Carly, who was herself a hairdresser. 'It was probably even longer when she was younger, down to her bum. Chantelle always said she'd never have colour put into her hair as it might ruin it. It wasn't until we left school that she started having highlights before going totally blonde. Now I think she could have a great TV career ahead of her.'

Throughout all this focus on Chantelle, interest remained high in the other contestants, especially Michael Barrymore. Once the undisputed king of prime-time television, he, like his fans, was clearly hoping that his stint on *Celebrity Big Brother* would mark the end of his exile in New Zealand, and allow him to resume his place in British society. The public was very keen to know what he had made of the whole experience, and he was happy to oblige. For Chantelle, he had nothing but praise.

'She fooled me completely,' he said. 'I thought she was an ex-member of Atomic Kitten, although I wondered why she didn't know the lyrics to her own hit record. I'm glad she won. She's perfect, absolutely adorable. I loved Chantelle. She was so natural and down-to-earth. I hope she stays that way, even though I think she will become famous now.'

He certainly didn't feel that way about all the other housemates, and Jodie, in particular, came in for some serious stick. The rows between them had actually cost Barrymore some goodwill when he was in the house, because he had appeared at times to be so unpleasant to her, but he was adamant that the public had not, by a long shot, been told the whole truth.

'The things she said about Jordan continuously were absolutely vile, just pure vulgarity, disgusting,' he said. 'Viewers never heard them because they were so bad they had to be edited out. That made it a bit unfair on me because people watching saw me have a rant at her but didn't know what had provoked it. She just wouldn't leave Jordan alone and I told her this game, showbusiness, is hard enough without slagging each other off. The row where I made her cry came after one particularly nasty attack on Jordan. It was vulgar and crude, just pure bile. I thought, Jodie's mum and dad are probably watching this and it is completely unacceptable. She is obsessive about her.'

Unsurprisingly, Barrymore was delighted when Jodie left. 'She was the first to have a dig at me over the Stuart Lubbock situation,' he said. 'I readied myself for the housemates bringing it up but I was surprised it was Jodie who did. I thought, Oh, here we go. What annoyed me was that she alluded to it, then bottled it, refusing to come straight out with it and give me the right to reply.'

Another housemate Barrymore was glad to see the back of was George. The two had initially got on, but

Galloway began to irritate his fellow celebs so much that they ended up calling him Captain Mainwaring, after the character in *Dad's Army*, because he was so irritating and officious.

'He was always ordering us around, talking to us as if he was on the podium making a speech,' Barrymore said. 'I won't go as far as to say I disliked George but I found him unbelievable in the end. He's this left-wing politician who's always on his soapbox about inequality but he seems to like the finer things in life. It was the clash over cigars that really irked me. I admit I smoke a lot and I needed cigarettes, especially in there. Big Brother told me in the Diary Room we could have a packet in exchange for a cigar.

'George had two boxes of those very expensive cigars he loved to smoke, those ones that look like Fidel Castro rolled them himself. I asked him for one but he refused, so I asked Dennis Rodman for one and, although he had less than George, he gave me one immediately. I don't like meanness. I am a very generous person. I will give anyone anything if I can. George I found mean-spirited and that is my pet hate in a person.'

Barrymore was not beyond being wildly entertained by George's more toe-curling moments in the show. The notorious cat footage was new to the inmates of the house, and Barrymore couldn't help but let out a howl of glee when asked about it. 'A cat? George looked more like an old tabby from Tower Hamlets,' he said. 'When they finally showed it to me, I laughed my head off. It was cringe-making – all that mewing.'

And he wasn't very impressed by Faria. 'She was always moaning about being famous, saying she couldn't handle the attention and I thought, What are you doing in here then?' Nor was he that keen on Dennis, not least because he couldn't understand his accent. 'The only word I ever did understand from Dennis was "motherfucker". He was always sat there muttering it. We did clash one day, in the kitchen. He had a go at me and I stood up to him, basically saying, "Are you threatening me?" I'm six foot three inches but he towers over me and I thought, Oh, God, he's going to thump me. But he backed down and walked off.'

What about Rula? 'In the house, she never stopped performing as if she was on stage,' said Barrymore. 'I don't think we ever saw the real Rula. She told me early on, "I really want to win. An actress has never won *Big Brother* before." I told her, "It's only a game, love." And she told me in a very luvvy voice, "It's a competition to the end." But I thought she was a very nice lady and I would love to work with her again.'

He was rather fascinated with Traci for another reason: her breasts. 'She was basically just a walking pair of boobs,' he said. 'They seemed to have a life of their own. Everything in the house with Traci revolved around her boobs. She was forever saying, "Oops" as a nipple popped out, then two seconds later it would be "Oops" again as the other one came out. It was always right in front of the cameras, so I don't think it was accidental. It was a bit of a waste her popping her nipples out in my direction anyway.'

But he did warm to Pete. 'I was terrified of him at first,' he said. 'He was this huge camp queen, with all the hair and make-up. But he has a very funny wit. I really like him.'

He also liked Preston and Maggot. 'They were a lot younger than me. I called them and Chantelle "the kids". I felt very protective of them. Maggot is great. He has a very dry wit. I think he's one to watch and will be big in the future. I really liked Preston, too. I thought it was nice he said he just wanted to be in *Big Brother* because he liked the show.'

And Barrymore clearly had no regrets about taking part. 'At stages it felt like one long continuous group-therapy session,' he said. 'It was interesting to see how the egos emerged and how some people lose the plot. My time in AA and rehab helped me. I used to say the serenity prayer from AA to get me through it. But most times I felt like the most normal person there. They were all desperate to win. I was just being myself and enjoying the experience.' And winning back the affections of some of the British public, to boot.

But it was Chantelle who remained the public's prime object of fascination. She had made such an impact on girls of her own generation that they were actually beginning to copy her look. Superdrug was one of the many companies that wanted to sign up Chantelle, in their case to give a make-up masterclass in shops all over the country, citing her as a massive influence on who was buying what. 'Since Christmas, we've been selling more and more bright colours,' said Simon Comins, the company's cosmetics buyer. 'But, since *Celebrity Big Brother*, the interest has rocketed. We've sold more green eye shadow in one week than the whole of last year. It can only be down to the Chantelle effect. It certainly isn't down to George Galloway!'

9

Famous and Loving It

Now it was the turn of George Galloway to talk about the recent past, and he started with the subject of Chantelle. He appeared to be mounting some kind of damage-limitation exercise, and being completely straightforward about his housemates and what had happened inside the house appeared to be the best way to go about it. His opinion of Chantelle was actually to change over the next few weeks, as he watched her taking off into the stratosphere, but, for now, at least, his opinion of her was not very high. And being Galloway, of course, he could not resist making a political issue out of it.

'I think she is what she seems and that is obviously

appealing up to a point, though slightly shocking that our education system is failing so,' he said, drawing attention to Chantelle's ignorance of the work of a gynaecologist and belief that Dundee was in South Wales. 'Living in Britain in 2006, that's surely extraordinary,' he said. 'A number of people thought maybe it was an act. I think the truth is more prosaic. I think she's 22 going on 15.'

He was also concerned that Chantelle might be led astray by Jodie Marsh. 'I said to her one night, "You don't want to make Jodie your role model. At the moment, the nation loves you. They won't love you if you start taking your clothes off and talking dirty like Jodie does."' He was right there. Jodie is to be pitied, more than anything else, for her behaviour, partly because she clearly has no idea how badly it comes across and partly because she must have some very unresolved issues to put herself about in the way that she does. But Chantelle, for all that she got on with Jodie in the house, was not about to do the same. She was to play her cards very cannily indeed over the next few months.

Galloway himself was still in a reflective mode, and he was more aware now of how his own behaviour had been seen. 'I forgive anyone who cursed me and I hope anyone I cursed forgives me,' he said. 'At the end of the day, it was only a game.'

But he still seemed unable to comprehend quite how savage the reaction to his own stage in the house had been. In fact, at the earliest opportunity, he got in touch with his agent Ron McKay to ask quite how bad it had been. 'It's been fucking grim,' came the reply.

'George was shell-shocked when I outlined what had happened when he was inside the house,' said McKay afterwards. 'But his interview with Davina went extremely well, which is something.'

As for Galloway himself, he was philosophical. 'But when you are down, the only way is up,' he said. 'I'm still surprised at a moment when one Lib Dem politician after another appears to be tumbling out of the closet that me doing a funny act for charity on TV got quite so much coverage. The response I've had from the public does not match the headlines.

'I had three goals – to raise money for a Palestine charity, to employ two new members of staff in my constituency and to reach a wider audience. I wanted to show a public that might only have heard of me as Mr Angry on demonstrations that I can sing and laugh and make people laugh. Only time will tell if I achieved that. If you believe the newspapers, then not. If you believe the anecdotal evidence, then I did.'

The makers of *Big Brother* had actually been

wooing him for some time. Peter Bazalgette had already spoken about getting the mix of people just right, and the inclusion of George Galloway was clearly a huge success. Like him or loathe him, Galloway's presence had brought a certain something to the proceedings that had resulted in some compelling television. The man himself, though, seemed to think that the producers had not been entirely straightforward with him. He had clearly been hoping to spend his time in the house making statesman-like pronouncements about politics, but instead he had not been allowed to get his political views across to a huge captive audience the whole time he was there.

'They said it would be an opportunity for me to project my point of view on the war,' said Galloway, who eventually was paid twice the £75,000 fee already on offer. 'I assumed things I was saying were appearing. Instead, I found out I was bleeped out. Some of it was inexplicable. I was discussing with Faria the way Islam is misrepresented in the press and it was censored. Another time I was recalling an anecdote about Enoch Powell, who told me, "Never enter the chamber without two verbal hand grenades," and that was cut out. He's now written out of history as a racist madman but there was more to Powell than that. I wouldn't have gone on the show if they had said I would be bleeped out every time I talked about politics. There was clear censorship and I'm angry about that.'

He went on to recall his rather odd introduction to the house. 'The first thing I saw were three exotic-looking dark women. It turned out only one of them was naturally tanned and that was Traci. Jodie was unnaturally tanned and the third was Pete. I'd never heard of Dead Or Alive – I think they were popular around the time of the miners' strike, so I was otherwise occupied.

'It's virtually impossible for anyone to really understand [the atmosphere of boredom in the house] unless they have been there. Each day is virtually identical and it has the desired effect – it means everyone is increasingly introspective, thinking no more about the outside. You end up doing little else but talking about each other. I'm not ashamed of anything I said and I meant everything I said. However, I do think that all of us got things out of proportion.'

Living conditions were also pretty horrible, he said. 'By the end of the stay, the house was beginning to smell – the air conditioning was smelling. One minute the house is too cold, the next too hot. It's too bright or too dark – that's Big Brother controlling everything. Not being able to read anything was the hardest thing. You can only read the back of a Fruit 'n' Fibre packet so many times. Towards the end, I was given the Communist Manifesto. I had read it many times before, of course, but devoured it like a starving man devours a fine meal. Another thing that surprised me was that very few, if any, of the other housemates were aware of the George Orwell book *1984*. I alluded to it many times but no one picked up on it.'

Galloway was completely blunt about his fellow housemates. 'My first impression was that it was a very uninteresting group of people,' he said. 'That turned out to be completely wrong.' He was especially thoughtful on the subject of Michael Barrymore. 'I was touched by his emotions and immediately formed a positive view about him,' he said. 'He's been monstrously ill-treated and should be able to work like any other artist. Yet that which touched me began to be wearing. He was candid enough to say, "I did nothing wrong except for being stupid."'

But ultimately it all went sour. 'I realised fairly quickly that there's something wrong about a man who is always performing,' said Galloway. 'He's an act more than he is a man. He intervenes before people can tell a story. He needs to be centre stage. I doubt if I saw much of the real man.'

Preston drew some cautious words from Galloway. 'I'm not sure we have seen the real Preston. He's posing as a mockney. I'm not sure how typical of a young generation that is.'

As for Pete, 'He's a brilliant man but he is often unforgivably cruel. He spares no one, with the exception of me, perhaps. The things he says to Chantelle are breathtaking. The next minute he's helping her with her make-up. I will be seeing him again after the show. I think he's close to genius.'

Galloway also remarked that he was aware that he didn't want to offend his Muslim supporters. 'When people were threatening to show each other their sex organs, that was a problem because I couldn't be in the room with that. It was mainly Jodie – she talked about, if she had a woman, what she would do with her. I certainly don't think I was bullying her. I had only one strong exchange with her – that doesn't count as bullying where I come from. I considered her about the most primitive woman I've ever met. I found no redeeming qualities about her. I knew she wasn't stupid and in a way that kind of makes it worse.'

But he did like Dennis Rodman enormously. 'I know he was superfit, and me and Maggot were far from fit,' he said of the occasion when the two did a bit of shadow boxing. 'He didn't want to take on the role as trainer – after all, he's an international sporting star. He would stroll over and surreptitiously look at our heart monitors or our inclines and say things like, "Take it easy there," then wander off again. I've got a lot of respect for him. I feel fondness for all of the housemates. I've realised not only do I not hate any of them, I don't dislike them either. Although in the house there were moments when I disliked them intensely.'

Amid it all, Chantelle attempted to keep her feet on the ground. She had no problem whatsoever with being an eligible bachelorette, but she warned gold diggers that she could see right through them. 'If you're after my money I'll rumble you,' she said. 'I'll be able to tell if anyone is trying to get to know me or use me just because I've won *Big Brother*. I'm not stupid. Right now, all I want to do is have a good time and enjoy what's happening in my life.'

She also revealed that it was because she'd had to stand up to bullies when she was younger that she'd been strong in the *Big Brother* house. 'Bullies made life hell,' she said. 'They'd call me names and pull my hair. But I wouldn't let them stop me from going somewhere. It made me stronger.'

The initial shock – and thrill – of winning had barely begun to wear off before serious thought

The love of her life: Samuel Preston, here arriving at the Brit Awards.

Above left: Preston's former girlfriend, Camille Aznar, who was reported to have been upset by the singer's flirting with Chantelle in the *Big Brother* house.

Above right: Preston arriving at the *NME* awards.

Below: Performing with his band, *The Ordinary Boys*.

The two lovebirds enjoy a stroll outside Preston's house.

The pair have certainly enjoyed being in the limelight – they are regulars at celebrity parties, and are pictured here at the Prada *GQ* party for the new *GQ* style mag.

they haven't forgotten their roots – here they are shopping at the market.

'I do!' Chantelle shows off her new sparkler at the *New Woman* beauty awards, when she announced her engagement to Preston.

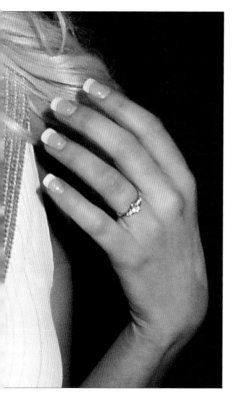

ve left: The ring in close-up.

ve right: The exclusive wedding shop in Hove, which Chantelle and Preston checked
hortly after announcing their engagement (*below*).

Showing off her moves. Chantelle celebrates her engagement on the dance floor.

began to go into how Chantelle should kick off her new career. Everyone involved was hoping that it might have some longevity, but obviously a certain amount of speed was needed while, to put it bluntly, everyone still knew who Chantelle was. And so it was entirely appropriate that someone who had become a celebrity overnight should be involved in something that made people into millionaires overnight, namely the EuroMillions lottery.

As it happened, the timing was perfect. The top prize had been rolling over every week since November, with the result that the jackpot now stood at £125 million, the largest ever. And so who better to promote it? 'Last Friday night proved to be lucky for Chantelle and we're crossing our fingers and hoping her luck will rub off on UK players in this Friday's EuroMillions draw,' said a spokesman for the lottery. 'The massive £125 million jackpot which is up for grabs could be just as life-changing for a UK winner as *Celebrity Big Brother* has proved to be for Chantelle.' And it was a perfectly respectable choice for Chantelle to make: her predecessors in the role included Nell McAndrew and Elizabeth Jagger.

It was shortly after this, in early February, that the inevitable happened: Preston and Camille split up. Only a week earlier, they'd got engaged, in a gesture that turned out to be Preston's attempt to patch up their relationship. But, in truth, a definitive break had been on the cards practically from the moment he and Chantelle first laid eyes on each other in the *Big Brother* house. Preston was keen, though, to emphasise that it was the media attention that had driven them apart, rather than his friendship with Chantelle. 'My girlfriend that I had, she doesn't want to be in the papers and everything,' he said on *GMTV*. 'It's basically made it totally impossible for me to go out with her. It's just horrible.' At the same time, he was emphatic that this did not mean he was about to run off with Chantelle. 'If I want to see Chantelle, even if I just want to see her to chat to her, everybody's going to be saying, "Oh, Preston and Chantelle are off in a dodgy meeting somewhere."'

His father, Anthony, was taken aback by the news. 'I haven't heard that at all,' he said. 'It doesn't tally with what I've been told… We heard about it for the first time shortly after he came out of the *Big Brother* house. To the family, it wasn't a huge surprise, simply because we had been expecting something like that for some time.' There was another complication when Vivien revealed that Chantelle had had a boyfriend for four years, who broke up with her shortly before she entered the *Big Brother* house. 'The bloke who did it doesn't even justify talking about,' she said. 'If Chantelle meets someone, she stays with them long term. But she's had her share of hurts and it's me that she turns to.'

Matters became even more murky when one Ricci Golding popped up, claiming to have been Chantelle's boyfriend for the past two months. 'Chantelle is mine and will stay mine – Preston should keep away from her,' he said. 'I am really annoyed by all the attention on those two, and he should just forget it. I am going to do my best to make things work with Chantelle. Preston can forget it if he thinks he's getting his hands on my Chantelle. She would never consider going out with him. We are really happy together and, although it's early days, I can see it lasting. She liked Preston as a friend and enjoyed his company in the house – but that's where it ended.'

Confusing as all this was, it did nothing to dent Chantelle's popularity with the public. Almost overnight, it seemed, she had also become a role model. The preparations for the seventh series of *Big Brother* were now under way and what all the potential contestants aspired to, of course, was to be the next Chantelle.

'She was such a natural and, like Jade Goody, she was very much herself,' said Paul Scott, the executive producer of *Big Brother*, who scoured the country looking for contestants for the show and acknowledged that Chantelle was now the person everyone wanted to emulate. 'Those are the people who tend to be successful in *Big Brother* – the people who aren't afraid of showing exactly who they are, warts and all. The thing about being in *BB* is you can't hide what you are. That's who you become – you become yourself in the house. So the most important thing is to be yourself and my main tip is do what you want to do or say to stand out and impress us.'

What might be termed the Chantelle effect was only too clear as the producers of *Big Brother* held the first round of auditions for the next series in London's St James's Park. More than a thousand hopefuls turned up for the new show, which was scheduled for the summer of 2006, doing all that they could to catch the producers' eyes. Paul and his fellow exec Claire O'Donohoe pronounced themselves impressed by the 'boisterous and excited' crowd that turned up, many doing all they could to catch the producers' eyes.

One, Anwar Haq, a 37-year-old who had travelled from York for the day, came dressed as Mr Darcy. 'This is my "Yes! Yes! Yes!" costume,' he said. 'Few refuse me when I'm wearing it.'

And Chantelle's name was everywhere. 'People have been mentioning Chantelle a lot during auditions,' said Paul. 'She is obviously an inspiration.'

'I was a huge fan of Chantelle's,' said Laura Peart, a 26-year-old student nurse from Newcastle. 'She was under tremendous pressure in a house filled with celebrities, but won by being herself.'

Dan Wilson, 17, from Killingworth, agreed. He said that 'being yourself' was more important than anything, and was even prepared to miss his A-levels if he got on the show. 'I'd rather have the fame than the qualifications,' he said.

Meanwhile, 'Monkey' Mike, 48, from Darlington, revealed, 'I almost made it last year,' as he played spoons to the crowd and distracted them by doing impressions of 1980s TV favourites Zippy and Bungle.

Now it was time for Maggot to muse on his time in the house. Like the others, his life at that time was so dominated by *Celebrity Big Brother* that everything he did and said made the news, including the fact that, when he and his band, Goldie Lookin Chain, put on a show at Liverpool's Carling Academy on Valentine's Day, he was encouraging people to come on stage to propose live to their partners.

Liverpool had a special place in Maggot's heart, as he had lived there when he was a student. And he had devised a way for people to get up on stage. 'You need to go up to the merchandise man and say, "Can you feel the love?"' he said. 'And we're going to let people get up on stage and propose.' Alas, he revealed, 'There is still no Mrs Maggot yet, though.'

But Newport's most famous export, who had come third in the show, was relieved to be out. 'It's nice to be back in the real world,' he said. 'There is a "Welcome Home Maggot" party in Newport planned for St David's Day. It was fun in the house, though. There were so many best bits it's hard to choose. Being invited to sleep with Traci was a highlight – I don't think I hid that. And Rula's meditation techniques were good. Who needs drugs when you've got her? I haven't done the meditation since I came out, though, because I haven't got the chimes. But it wasn't very nice at times with all the bickering and arguing and moderate amounts of bullying. I don't like that.'

And now Goldie Lookin Chain, a sort of spoof band, was to take to the road again. It emerged that the makers of *Celebrity Big Brother* had actually produced the band as a whole and asked them to choose a member to go on the show. Maggot, said his band members, was the obvious choice. 'We chose Maggot because we thought he would be the best at it,' said band member Mystical. 'It's been great watching him on telly. When things happen in there, you do get worried. We were wondering if he was eating OK and whether he was happy because he's normally an opinionated bastard. It's like watching our pet guinea pig running round in a cage. We wanted him to shine but we were worried because he's all our own Maggot.'

Maggot was never won round by Galloway, who he thought should have been doing his job in the Commons – 'It's all right for me. I'm in a band and nothing really happens in January' – but he did confess to revising his thoughts about Barrymore. 'I think my allegiances were very obvious in the show,' he said. 'You could see I was a bit hesitant of Michael at the start but I gave him the benefit of the doubt and he came across as a very funny man.'

As for coming third, he was 'a bit surprised to tell you the truth. I was still on the winners' podium and I had a great reaction when I walked out – there was a great amount of goodwill out there. When I was in the house and it was down to six of us, I was asked who I thought would win and I said Michael or Chantelle, so I wasn't surprised about that. It was quite nerve-racking going in there – it's tough. At first, you're really conscious of the cameras but that goes.'

He had been right about Chantelle winning, but he was not entirely correct about everything to do with her, particularly her relationship with Preston. 'I don't think it was a romance,' he said. 'I think a lot of people are making something out of nothing. They had a strong bond and formed a good friendship but that's it really.

'I've still got very strong connections to Liverpool,' he continued. 'Way back in the 1990s, yes, way back, I was at university there. I only went for one year and I didn't really go. I don't know what I did really.'

But he was looking forward to the new gigs. After Liverpool came the London Astoria, but it was the Carling Academy gig, he said, that he was really looking forward to. 'I really love Liverpool, though,' he said. 'I'm not just saying that. I love the place – it's a great city. My old mate Pete [Burns, a Liverpudlian] will be invited but I don't know if he'll come – I doubt it.'

Other recent *Big Brother* inmates were still smarting from it all. George Galloway was beginning a fairly impressive fightback against the mauling he'd had about his time in the house, responding to the outcry about his most notorious moment by saying, 'I'd rather be a pussycat than George Bush's poodle. He seemed to have decided that the best way to limit the damage was to confront it head on. 'I obviously regret some of the things I said – or more the strength of what I said,' he admitted. 'I got unnaturally angry about my voting rights being taken away from me and I shouldn't have. It wasn't that important.' As for the leotard, 'I knew that there would be a certain price that had to be paid for being on the show. I knew there would be an indignity or two along the way. You have a total lack of proportion and perspective in the house. We were locked up 24/7 in a laboratory, like laboratory guinea pigs. I put all external matters out of my mind – that might have been a mistake.'

And of the charge that he had been neglecting his constituents, Galloway was scathing. 'Sanctimonious humbug!' he said. 'MPs are flying all over the world on fact-finding missions to exotic places every fortnight. I didn't go to the Maldives or the Seychelles or on a parliamentary junket. I went on British TV to reach British people and my constituency office was fully staffed throughout. I'm feeling quite sanguine. I had three goals and I have already achieved two of them.'

Chantelle, by contrast, was having no problem whatsoever in reaching out to a wider audience. The first really significant breakthrough in her newfound celebrity status came when she was given her own programme on E4 called *Chantelle: Living the Dream*, for which she was to be paid £50,000. Appropriately enough, the subject of the series was none other than Chantelle herself: a camera crew was to follow her progress as she began to step out into her new showbiz world.

'We're going to see if Chantelle can really launch a pop career – maybe with her fake band Kandyfloss,' said an insider on the show. 'We're also going to follow her as she is launched on London's top nightspots. Can she pull a footballer, or will she end up with *BB* housemate Preston?'

But, wherever there is success, a backlash surely follows. And the first person to adopt the role of the Bad Fairy at the feast was, of all people, her former housemate Traci. Whether it was jealousy that Chantelle, a non-celeb, had not only triumphed over the others but was now doing extremely well, or the fact that she was telling it like it is, Traci was none too complimentary about her former friend.

'Chantelle was a sweet, kind-hearted girl in the *Big Brother* house, but the stardom has obviously changed her,' she said. 'She ignored me completely at the after-show wrap party on Monday night and wouldn't say anything to me. I was shocked at her behaviour. She looked me straight in the eye and just turned away. I think it's all gone to her head.

'Chantelle isn't an actress or a presenter, she's just a pretty girl who looks like a socialite. She doesn't even have her own image. She'll probably get some more work pretending to be Paris Hilton or promo jobs, but what else is there for her to do? I doubt she'll make it big anywhere else. She's not going to be an international star. The British public will probably have forgotten all about her by this time next year.' It was the first sour note from a fellow celebrity, rather casting a dampener on it all, but it was by no means the last.

Nor was Chantelle herself exactly complimentary about her erstwhile housemates, saving her wrath, in particular, for George. 'George was a horrible, horrible, horrible man at times, and I won't ever forgive him for calling Preston malicious, vile and scheming,' she said during one of her numerous media appearances, this one on *The Brendan Courtney Show* in Ireland. 'I felt as though George thought I was a stupid girl.' Given the difference in the way both had been greeted in their emergence from the house and subsequent fortunes, it was quite a mistake for George to make.

Meanwhile, will they or won't they? Were they or weren't they? Chantelle and Preston were remaining remarkably coy. Preston even admitted to encouraging the ongoing speculation about the real state of play between him and his new friend. 'I quite like the fact that everyone speculates,' he said. 'I contradict myself in every interview just to keep the myth going.'

It wasn't that hard to read between the lines, though. Of Camille, he said, 'The thing is, she doesn't want to be a celebrity, hounded by the press.'

And Chantelle? 'I was literally biting my lip until it bled to try not to cry when she won.'

There was even greater speculation about what was really going on when the pair were spotted staying overnight in a London flat belonging to a friend of Preston. But, still, the two stayed shtum.

Next up, they were seen at the achingly trendy White Cube Gallery in London's Hoxton at an exhibition of works by the controversial avant-garde artists Gilbert and George. 'They arrived on their own and Preston was showing Chantelle around,' said someone who had seen them enter. 'At one stage, he was overheard whispering to her, "They're really famous artists, you know."' Then Chantelle appeared in the audience at the London Astoria, where the Ordinary Boys were performing, dancing along as Preston appeared to sing 'Be My Baby' just for her.

That was not all. Chantelle appeared on the children's show *Holly and Stephen's Saturday Showdown* and was asked to choose between Blue's Simon Webbe and Jade's ex, Jeff Brazier. 'I can't – I'm off limits,' she replied. She was then asked if she had got a Valentine's card from Preston and said,

'No.' Shortly afterwards, a lie-detector test told the audience that this wasn't quite true.

Just friends? It was an act that was increasingly hard to keep up. Shortly before jetting off to Japan with the Ordinary Boys, Preston took Chantelle and her mother out for dinner, during which the two couldn't keep their hands off each other. It was the fact that they'd been spotted that finally seemed to compel the two of them to let everyone else in on the world's worst-kept secret. Yes, they were a couple. And they were in love.

As so often happens in these cases, once they started talking about it, they couldn't stop. It is, after all, completely natural for a couple to want to share their happiness with the rest of the world, and this Chantelle and Preston now appeared to be doing in spades. Understandably, the fact that they'd had to keep it a secret for a while only intensified the joy of finally being able to talk about it.

'It's all true,' said Chantelle. 'We are together. It's brilliant. This is for keeps. It's amazing! We can finally be open about how we feel. It's been really hard trying to keep my feelings a secret since coming out of the house because I didn't want to upset Camille. But, now they have split up, we are an item and I couldn't be happier. I have found my soulmate in Preston and this is definitely for keeps.

Preston gets on really well with my mum. She thinks he's great.

'I'm so happy about everything. My life is just so brilliant at the moment. It's all like a dream come true. I think he's amazing. It is so great to finally be able to be a proper couple. All this time I have had to play down how I feel but now at last we can be upfront about it. It's fantastic and I just want to tell the world how happy I am. I don't know any woman out there who doesn't fancy him. I reckon everyone in the country has a soft spot for Preston.'

10

The Beat Goes On

All the world loves a lover, and this was certainly true for Chantelle and Preston. The couple were offered £100,000 to tell their story to a magazine, putting that initial £25,000 Chantelle earned well and truly in the shade. She had by now agreed to record 'I Want It Right Now' and the filming of *Chantelle: Living the Dream* was going well. There was talk of her launching her own clothing range. If she had appeared happy before, that was nothing compared with how she was now, although it did seem that one person was on her conscience – Camille.

Preston's ex didn't seem entirely happy with the situation and who could blame her? A break-up is painful at the best of times and, in this case, it was being played out in the full glare of publicity. Camille wouldn't have been human if it hadn't rankled. 'There is nothing I can put down to express my feelings about that nymphomaniac,' she snapped. 'It is not possible he could ever marry that girl.' And as for herself having been seen out with a new man, 'I got fed up with it and now I am going out for a drink with someone else,' she said.

This produced a response from Chantelle. She was neither an unkind nor an unfeeling woman, and she was perfectly capable of understanding that Camille was bound to be feeling livid. To apologise in person was out of the question – odds are that Camille would have refused to see her – but she did at least do the next best thing, to try to make amends through the pages of a magazine. And these days it seemed as if Chantelle's life was being lived out in the pages of a magazine, such was the enormous interest shown in her, and so it was as apt a place as any to state her case.

'I just want her to know that no one went out to hurt anyone – it just sort of happened,' she said. 'She knows that it wasn't completely and utterly my fault. But things happen to people that completely change their lives. I mean, you could be married and go to the baker's because you're feeling hungry, then fall in love with the baker. Things happen that are unpredictable. He never had an affair or cheated. Circumstances made them split, and then this happened between us.'

And, in truth, she was so happy with Preston that she was scarcely able to think about anything else. 'It's just really lovely being with him,' she said. 'We're just going to spend some time together and see what happens. We're really happy.'

After a while, Camille began to calm down as far as Chantelle was concerned, but she clearly remained unhappy with Preston. 'I could see Chantelle was flirting with Preston... maybe I was naive, but I decided to trust him,' she said.

'We got engaged but the pressure on us was so tough we decided to call it off... we could never go back to how we were. It has been very difficult going through a break-up and seeing your boyfriend with another woman. I've had to take compassionate leave from my job because of the stress. I don't hold anger towards Chantelle. I'm not a victim. [But] I'm not sure Preston realises what it's been like for me.'

But Camille was not the only person who had been rather dismayed by Chantelle's arrival on the scene. Other people in the industry were not exactly thrilled either, primarily those who were also reality-television stars and were concerned she was taking their crown. Chantelle's ex-housemate Traci had already voiced a few rather cautious remarks, and now it was the turn of the queen of reality TV herself, Jade Goody, to do likewise.

'Jade is deeply concerned that her work – and money – is going to dry up now Chantelle has captured the nation's heart,' said a source close to the lady herself. 'She has had meetings with her agent to discuss how she can boost her profile and stay in the limelight. Jade has had a great run but Chantelle is a big name and it looks like she's here to stay. Jade is worried no one will be interested in her any more. She has made a fortune out of appearing in glossy mags but now Chantelle is the girl everyone wants. And Chantelle has the Jordan and Peter Andre-style romance with Preston to help keep her in the headlines for longer.'

Jade, incidentally, was the supreme example of what a reality-television star could achieve. She was estimated to have earned over £1 million since coming to prominence in *Big Brother* in 2002, and has been in and out of the headlines ever since. To this day, she is seen as the person for those who aspire to be a *Big Brother* housemate to look up to and, if Chantelle emulates her success even without overtaking it, she will be a successful woman indeed.

By contrast, another reality-TV star was rather

complimentary, and it's a fair bet that this was the compliment that Chantelle relished most. It came from none other than Paris Hilton herself, who thoroughly approved of her wannabe – although she couldn't resist making a slight dig at the same time. 'I love her. She's hot and sexy,' said Paris. 'We have got a lot in common looks-wise. I have a lot of people that look like me all over the world, but she's one of the better ones – she's working it. I'd love to meet her. It's not easy being me [though] and she'll have to work hard to keep up the look.'

To date, Chantelle has done just that.

It was another of the couple's former housemates, Maggot, who was the first to go public with the expectation that this relationship would go all the way. 'Preston will marry… in a kilt,' he said. 'I'll be best man. And I'd definitely be happy to sing. I reckon Preston will wear a kilt even though he's not Scottish. I dunno why. Maybe because he can't find his trousers.'

And he was positive about their future together. 'He's never going to cheat on her,' he said. 'She's had boyfriends who've taken advantage of her good nature in the past and done the dirty. But Preston will not do that. I'm really happy for them and Preston will be really decent to her. He's a put-your-feet-up-and-cook-a-nice-meal kind of guy.'

Someone else who was delighted by her relationship with Preston and her growing fame was Chantelle's father. 'I always knew she would be famous,' said Alan in his first proper interview about his daughter. 'She's very single-minded and always wanted to do something special.'

Alan had a theory: that it was his divorce from Vivien that gave Chantelle, then 15, the determination to become a star. 'The split was completely amicable, but it had a marked effect on Chantelle,' he said. 'She learned a lot from the divorce, it made her stronger. Chantelle was upset, but we kept it close as a family. She dealt with it very maturely and helped me by staying close to me. Chantelle wouldn't pre-judge either of us. She never took sides. She realised that mum and dad fell out of love and it was better for the family for us to be apart.'

He remembered his daughter when very young with great affection. 'As a baby, she had a nice colour – she tans very well,' he said. 'She looked quite dark and quite lovely. She was always a very friendly and dainty little girl. Later she did the majorettes and loved dressing up.'

Alan watched his daughter growing up with pride, although he admitted her brief stint as a Page 3 girl was a little bit hard to take. 'As a parent, you are obviously going to think, Oh, my God, my child's in there topless!' he said. 'As a father you can't be comfortable with it. All I said was, "So long as it's only topless and it's tasteful."'

But the two always remained close, although they had not yet had a proper chance to catch up. Chantelle had been so swamped with work and offers, and so generally overwhelmed by her new existence, that she had not had much time to see her father. 'We saw a lot of each other but since *CBB* we've only managed to snatch a coffee and toast in the back of my cab,' Alan said. 'It's very difficult now for her to go out, but as soon as it's quiet we'll have a nice meal and some father–daughter time.'

And while *Big Brother* itself was actually running, Alan only had one moment in which he was concerned about his child. It was when Chantelle was called upon to sing. 'She's not really a singer,' he said delicately. 'I've heard her sing to the radio in my cab and she's a bit tone-deaf. When she had to sing in *CBB*, I thought, Oh! But she was really confident.'

And he worked out what was happening with Preston from the start. 'Being a man, I could see from the body language he was attracted to her,' he said. 'They were the two sanest people there and they clicked. Chantelle likes the way he dresses, he's clean-cut and happy-go-lucky, with a smile on his face. He's a normal young fella and – in my eyes – a lucky one. It must have been very difficult for him in the house, having feelings for Chantelle but knowing his girlfriend was watching. Preston could try to pretend it wasn't happening but anyone could see it. At times, you can't help who you fall in love with, it's one of life's wonders. They clicked because he gained her trust very quickly. Chantelle's had a couple of boyfriends where it hasn't worked out and she finds it very hard to trust them.'

As for the future, Alan was hopeful. 'People say to me it will only last three months. But I'm convinced she will last a lot longer,' he said. 'She's far more intelligent than people give her credit for, a very mature girl with an older head on her shoulders. I've known for years that my daughter's a star. But now it is wonderful that the public have taken Chantelle to their heart and realised she is a star, too.'

And so the momentum continued to mount. Far from being a seven-day wonder, Chantelle continued to fascinate people, to the extent that there were now talks about none other than Paris Hilton appearing on her TV show *Living the Dream*. 'I think it could happen and it would be so exciting to meet her,' said Chantelle. 'Basically, it's a case of "my people are talking to her people" and we'll see what happens.'

If truth be told, Chantelle was beginning to want to

be thought of as more than a Paris Hilton lookalike. It had been all very well to begin with and had, after all, given her an entry into the house, but as she became increasingly well known in her own right she no longer wanted recognition just for her resemblance to someone else. There were even talks about trimming those long blonde locks, although what Preston might have said about that is not on record. But the main point was, Chantelle now had her own career to pursue.

And her new romance was going from strength to strength – although her father did have a warning for Preston when it came to his little girl. Asked what would happen if Preston ditched Chantelle the way he did Camille, Alan replied, 'If he did that to Chantelle, he wouldn't be popular with me. If any man did the dirty on her, he'd have me to answer to. She's my little girl and I'll look out for her.'

She was his increasingly wealthy little girl, too. That £25,000 she earned on leaving the *Big Brother* household was beginning to look like peanuts compared with what she'd earned since leaving the house. In March, it was reported that she'd earned a staggering £750,000 from work that included promoting the EuroMillions jackpot, her television series and a fashion shoot with Marks & Spencer. 'She is amazed by what she is earning, and how people react when they see her, but she is very down-to-earth and enjoying every minute of it,' a source close to her said. 'Chantelle knows it might not last forever, but she has got a great career and the boyfriend she always wanted.'

It was one up to the bosses on *Big Brother*. Someone rather cruelly leaked the notes made on Chantelle in preparation for the show, in which the programme chiefs said she was 'a bimbo' and 'wants to be strong and independent but probably isn't'. She could be a 'giggler', they also noted – although by this time she was giggling all the way to the bank.

Another possibility was an appearance on prime-time soap opera *Hollyoaks*. Chantelle herself was enormously keen on the idea, saying, 'I dream of having a career where I get to do lots of varied things. I am really hoping I get the chance to go into *Hollyoaks*, even if it's just for a guest slot. I really love the show.' It looked as if it might be on the cards. 'I understand approaches have been made to her but it's still early days,' said a source. 'Even if she just came and did a few episodes, we're sure that the show's army of fans would go crazy for her.'

And people did go crazy for Chantelle wherever she turned. Young girls, in particular, adored her and would mob her whenever she went out. Matters got so out of hand during a trip to London's Brent Cross

Shopping Centre that she had to lock herself in a changing room. 'She wasn't shopping, but she did hide in the Reiss changing rooms, so she could get away from the little girls who wanted her autograph,' said an onlooker. 'She just wanted some peace.'

More extraordinary still was the next issue of the *Times Literary Supplement*. The cover featured a colour shot of Chantelle licking her lips, not the sort of image normally associated with a magazine aimed at a small highbrow readership. The reason for it was an article by Marshall McLuhan entitled 'The Medium is the Message'. Her appearance here, of all places, showed just how far Chantelle had infiltrated the national consciousness.

And, as her career continued to flourish, so did Preston's. The latest gig to come his way was on Virgin Radio: he signed up for four three-hour Sunday-afternoon shows to chat to guests and play music. 'Being in a band means music is a massive part of my life,' he said. 'The chance to be a DJ on a station like Virgin is one in a million. I can't wait.'

Virgin was keen, too. 'Preston has established himself as a great media personality,' said Paul Jackson, Virgin's programme director. He had indeed, as had his girlfriend, whom he had taken along to the meeting with Virgin bosses. Together, they were far more than the sum of their parts. One of them alone was pretty good, but put the two together and they radiated youth, energy and, above all, possibility. Two ordinary people, they were now leading extraordinary lives. In a poll for the UK's favourite 'Prince Charming and Cinderella', which was won by Prince William and Kate Middleton, Chantelle and Preston came in at a creditable number five.

Could things get any stranger? Yes, they could. The latest wheeze was to promote Chantelle not as the new Paris Hilton but the new Barbara Windsor, as it emerged that she was being seriously considered for a role in a new Carry On film, *Carry On London*. 'Chantelle will brighten up the screen, she's such a pretty girl,' said an insider on the film, which was being written by *Comic Strip* star and writer Peter Richardson and was potentially to star David Walliams and Matt Lucas. 'Babs had her laugh and her boobs. It's given the crew a real boost to know she's getting involved.'

Chantelle really was having a fantastic time of it. Offers were flooding in and, while the attention might have seemed a little overwhelming at times, the opportunities were enormous. 'She is having the absolute time of her life and really has been living the dream, as she promised, since getting out of the house,' said a friend. 'She's so excited about all the opportunities that have been coming her way but the talk of a Carry On movie is one of the best. She's always been a fan. As people saw in the house, she loves cheeky humour, has a dirty laugh that could rival Barbara's and certainly has the looks for film. She's looking at it as another great experience that could open a few more doors. The chance of working with two of the funniest men ever is brilliant.'

Her appearance certainly was an enormous asset to her and, while Chantelle was careful to keep up the glam image at all times, she admitted that she didn't have to make a huge effort to retain her figure and was actually one of the lucky ones who didn't need to diet at all. 'I can pretty much eat what I like and not put weight on,' she said. 'I have never followed a diet, ever. In fact, earlier I was having a good old munch on a Toblerone! If I'm on the go and it gets to the point when I'm starving, I'll have some chocolate.'

She was also a proponent of the fuller figure, rather than the emaciated shape favoured by so many of today's celebs. 'Kelly Brook has an amazing figure. I just love her curves. She's so shapely,' Chantelle said. 'She's a great example to real women around the country. She proves that curves are really sexy. I'm not skinny, I'm curvy, but I think that's the best way to be. Womanly. It's sexy.'

Not everyone was bowled over by her, though. She was singled out by the Reverend Michael Trodden of Ampthill, Bedfordshire, for her constant use of the phrase 'Oh, my God'. But much of the country continued to be charmed, all the more so when rumours began to circulate that she and Preston might even be making wedding plans. Rumours intensified when the couple were spotted checking out a five-star hotel in Watford called the Grove, complete with a luxury spa.

'The Grove is always heaving with stars but Chantelle caught everybody's attention because she was so friendly,' said an onlooker. 'She was chatting to everyone. After trying out the spa, she had lunch with Preston before they looked at the various suites for functions. They really liked the Ivory Rooms but thought them a little small and eventually decided to check availability for the Amber Suite.

'It's a gorgeous room that can accommodate up to 400 people and it opens up on to the Grove's amazing gardens. They were quite coy about their plans but really excited to discover that the room was free on a couple of Saturdays in July and one in August. Everyone remarked on how in love they seemed and also just what a nice young couple they are. There's a real buzz about them getting married in the hotel.'

And Chantelle was also putting her celebrity to

good use. She helped launch an anti-bullying campaign, Bullywatch London, spurred on by her own experiences as a child. 'I was bullied when I was at school and I wish someone would have said, "Hang on, that's not acceptable," and it would have stopped,' she said. 'No one really knew about it but it got to the point where I didn't really go to school much. I would dread going to school. It's really important to tell someone in authority if you see someone being bullied. Too many people are ignoring it. And ignoring it can be as bad as doing it.' It was quite an event: Chantelle was joined by 130 schoolchildren from Manor Park Primary School and various members of the great and good for the launch, and together they released 130 balloons into the sky.

There was, alas, a rather sour note behind all this. Jodie Marsh had also been approached to lead a campaign, Beatbullying, as she, too, had been bullied at school. She had also, in many eyes, been bullied on *Big Brother* and had written of her housemates on her website that they were 'vile, egotistical, two-faced scheming twats'. And she'd had a go at Chantelle, saying, 'You need a brain, talent and personality to survive in this industry.'

When it was announced that Jodie would be fronting the campaign, there was an outcry, partly because her image was considered unsuitable to be wafted in front of children and partly because of the comments she'd posted on her website. The Liberal Democrat spokesman Phil Willis was appalled by it all. 'We looked at her weblog and what she'd written about her *Big Brother* housemates is just appalling,' he said. 'It is the language of an appalling bully. Is this really someone we want to send into schools? We are really descending to the lowest common denominator when we are putting people like her on a pedestal.' Jodie was unavailable for comment.

On a rather lighter note, a meeting of minds was now arranged between Chantelle and that other *Big Brother* success story Jade Goody. Jade interviewed Chantelle and the two touched on all the important topics of our times. Early on, she tackled the delicate subject of Preston dumping Camille and taking up with Chantelle. 'Can a leopard change its spots?' she asked. 'Aren't you scared Preston might leave you for someone else?'

'What do you mean?' said Chantelle. 'I don't know any leopards.'

They moved on to the alleged tensions between the two of them. 'The press are obviously pitching us as rivals,' said Jade. 'What do you say about that?'

'We're not rivals, are we?' asked Chantelle. 'How do you feel about it, Jade?'

'I don't see you as a rival, I see you as a big success and I hope you carry on doing well,' said Jade. 'Right, that's enough of the brown-nosing.'

Other revelations included the fact that the most Chantelle had spent on designer clothing was £180 on a pair of Diesel jeans, that her nightmare housemate would have been Makosi from a previous series of *Big Brother*, that her only regret in the house was eating and drinking everything in the secret *BB* room and that, within four years, she hoped to be a presenter.

And she managed to keep much of what should be private between her and Preston exactly that. Despite a good deal of teasing from Jade, all she revealed was that they did not get together as a couple until he'd split from Camille, that their first date was spent talking because they had a lot to talk about, that they clicked the moment they first met in the house and that she was thoroughly excited about the last few months. As well she might be, for her rise to fame was even more spectacular than Ms Goody's.

As for Preston, the conversation ran as follows: 'Did you do a lot of boshing [on your first date]?' Jade asked.

'Pardon? What does that mean?' replied Chantelle. Jade explained.

'Oh, I haven't even kissed him!' she said.

'So was your first Valentine's together a passionate night and the first time you boshed each other?' Jade continued.

'I don't understand,' said Chantelle wisely. 'We spent Valentine's together. I haven't spoken about what we did and I don't intend to.' It was a very sound policy.

This episode did confirm that Chantelle and Jade were now the two leading ladies of reality TV. The duo were among a number of *Big Brother* stars approached by bosses at the show *Celebrity X Factor* with a view to taking on *Big Brother* itself when it began its next series. The idea was that successful *BB* contestants had already been tried and tested and so were sure to make good television and push up the viewing figures.

'It might seem cheeky but we think some of the best contestants we could get for *X Factor* would be from previous *Big Brother* shows,' explained an ITV source. 'Chantelle is one of the most famous British women at the moment. She's made it clear that she would like to become a singer so this is a great chance for her to work with some of the biggest names in the industry. It's years since Jade has been on *Big Brother* but she is more popular now than ever. So it would be great if she appeared. She has

Living the dream! Chantelle finishes a hard day's filming on her latest television show, *Chantelle's Dream Dates*.

Flowers in hand, she exits the Radio 1 studios.

t the 2006 British Book Awards, where she presented the Best Debut Fiction award.

As a genuine celebrity Chantelle regularly mixes with the rich and famous –
here with Jamie Oliver.

th fellow reality TV winner Kerry Katona.

Above: Chantelle even gets the chance to mix with royalty! Here at the Prince's Trust 30th Birthday with the Prince of Wales.

Below: But she never forgets where she comes from – here with her sister and mother, Vivian

r proud father, Alan Houghton.

Chantelle gears up for a summer of fun at the *T4 On the Beach* event.

already been on *Stars In Their Eyes* and was a big success. We're not sure what Channel 4 will think if Chantelle and Jade come on the show. But we don't really care as long as we get good ratings.'

But events moved on fairly swiftly when it emerged that Chantelle was to get her own show. She had already filmed *Chantelle: Living the Dream*, but that was a one-off with fairly limited potential. Now, though, she was given the type of show that could have attracted an already established presenter, a move that showed quite how far she'd come in a very short time. She was to host *Dream Dates* for E4, in which she was to help singletons find love, partly by giving advice on dating and partly by helping them with their appearance. It was quite a coup. 'At the start of the year, Chantelle was a nobody,' said a source on the programme. 'Now she's fronting her own show. It has been an amazing transformation. A year ago, it was the sort of programme she might apply to go on.' Indeed it was – and now she'd beaten the competition to front it herself.

It was also the right sort of work for her to do. While Chantelle had no real scandals in her past, there was the small matter of having been a Page 3 girl some time back, and so the work she did had to be treated with care. As she herself put it, 'I want to do more TV work because I'm looking to get into presenting. I can't do kids' TV because I've had my baps out. I'm not doing any more topless shots and I haven't done for a long time.'

As Chantelle-mania continued to sweep the country, she and everyone around her continued to play up to her image. The world and his wife knew that her favourite colour was pink, and so she was presented with a pink limousine to whisk her around the country when filming her new series. 'She couldn't stop giggling when she saw the car – she was thrilled,' said an insider on the series.

And matters continued to go swimmingly with Preston. The two were now living in his flat and were spotted hunting for engagement rings, while there were also rumours that they planned to have matching tattoos. 'As long as it's discreet and classy, I will have it done, too,' said Chantelle.

There was another rather iffy moment when Chantelle came third in a list of Britain's most pointless celebrities (Fran Cosgrave came first, followed by Jodie Marsh), a finding that was slightly tempered by the fact that 44 per cent of those surveyed would also like to be famous themselves. It actually made quite amusing reading: Dr Glenn Wilson, a psychologist from King's College London, analysed the survey of a thousand adults and found that there were four key personality factors that both famous people and wannabes had in common: charisma, determination, exhibitionism and ruthlessness.

'The results show that many desire fame but the required qualities really only belong to a small minority,' he said. 'We have made the Fame Potential calculator available online at www.thorpepark.com/fame so that everyone can work out their own star quality.' It is difficult to conceive of Chantelle being ruthless, but she certainly fitted the bill in other ways, not least when it came to determination. By now, it was beyond doubt that, for her, taking part in *Celebrity Big Brother* was neither a whim nor a one-off: she had been actively seeking celebrity for some years now and it had finally come her way.

What had been a truly sensational debut on the national stage was capped by an event that had been on the cards for some time: Chantelle and Preston announced at last that they were engaged. The news broke in April at the *New Woman* Beauty Awards at the Dorchester Hotel in London, which Chantelle attended wearing an engagement ring. It was Preston's mother's wedding ring and had been 'in the family for quite a while'.

11

The Perfect Couple

Even though it had been widely speculated upon, Chantelle seemed quite overwhelmed by actually being engaged to Preston. Everything had happened so fast that she could be forgiven for thinking it was a dream: in such a short time to have acquired both celebrity status and a fiancé was a coup. 'It was as much unexpected for me as it was for him, you know,' she said. 'He asked for his mum to send the ring over, which she done and, you know, he asked me. It just happened. I just want to marry him. I've had a really long day today but I don't feel tired and I'm just dying to get home to see him.'

And, of course, she had already told her family and

friends. 'It was literally in half an hour,' she said. 'I rang my mum and everyone and we went to get a bottle of champagne and we celebrated.' As well she might. She revealed that the wedding would take place later in the year, but was a little coy about how Preston proposed and what all the exact details would be. And yet, had this been written up as a film script, the engagement would have fitted exactly with the way Chantelle's life was now taking shape. She had become famous by being on a reality-TV show and she had met Preston on the very same show. It seemed the perfect culmination of a life lived intentionally in the public eye.

Everything Chantelle did, wore or said immediately made the news: in a strange way, she was almost an everyman figure for our times. Quite apart from fulfilling Andy Warhol's prediction that in the future everyone would be famous for 15 minutes, Chantelle had achieved what is the ultimate to so many people – celebrity. It is as if, in this post-religious age, recognition in life will make up for loss of belief in anything after it. Fame has become the common goal. After all, Chantelle's parents had been thrilled when their daughter won *Big Brother*, not because she had actually achieved anything, but because her name had become a household word in the land.

She was even comparing her present situation to Cinderella's. 'All the photo shoots and make-up and going places and being picked up in really posh cars and being on TV – it's like a whirlwind. I don't ever want to turn into a pumpkin and I won't ever leave my shoes anywhere.'

And she was now so popular that babies were being named after her and Preston. 'There was something in a newspaper a few weeks back saying there was a baby boom of kids starting to be called Chantelle and Preston. So it'll be nice, won't it?' she said.

As for Preston, 'I just feel totally content the whole time,' he said deliriously (and a tad tactlessly, given Camille). 'I didn't know it could be as good as this. Chantelle's so relentlessly upbeat. She's so great for me, honestly. She just puts everything into perspective.' Actually, Preston might well have been aware of Camille's situation, for he had by now sold the flat in which they had lived together. Instead, he bought a £400,000 three-bedroom duplex flat in Brighton, just five minutes' walk from the sea. 'Chantelle had no idea – he plans to show it to her this week,' said a friend. 'She'll be over the moon. It shows how much he loves her.'

Her growing celebrity did, though, bring Chantelle the odd problem. Her new engagement ring, studded with six diamonds, was slightly too tight, but she didn't want to appear ringless while it was altered in case people decided that the engagement was just a publicity stunt. So she decided to find an alternative ring. 'She and her minders have been trying to find a fake,' said a source on her television show. 'She's so desperate not to cause a scare, so she'll probably settle for a plastic gem from a high-street store.'

Oh, the woes of celebrity! And note that comment about the minders. It was still unclear how long Chantelle's fame would last, but famous she was for the moment – probably as much as anyone in the country today. But she was coping remarkably well. Although there were a few snide remarks about it going to her head, Chantelle had become popular in the first place because she came across as a nice, straightforward girl from Essex, and that is the image she has managed to hold on to.

She came across both as a famous person in her own right and someone who was thrilled at what had happened to her and tremendously excited about all the people she was now going to meet. In other words, she appeared to her countless admirers to be exactly the same as them, but with the one proviso that she was, as she put it, living the dream. She did not appear to be spoiled, and continued to be friendly to just about everyone. She seemed a thoroughly likeable girl.

Preston certainly thought so. The two had become one of Britain's most popular couples, in demand everywhere and lauded at enormous lengths in the newspapers and magazines. And why not? They were young, cute and in love, and wanted the world to know it. They were almost like two small children, such was their innocent delight in the world and each other. And there was plenty more to come.

But there was still the odd word of caution. Michael Barrymore, no less, warned the two that it might be a mistake to rush into marriage, given that everything had happened so fast. He was surprised, he said, and added, 'You can get attracted by lucrative offers for your wedding pictures and get married for the wrong reason.'

This advice was clearly kindly meant. Barrymore had stayed in touch with the two: he had been invited to the wedding and was also going to appear with Chantelle on a celebrity version of *The Weakest Link*. But Chantelle and Preston were in no mood to wait: utterly swept up in the moment, they wanted to wed as soon as they could.

And still offers continued to roll in. Chantelle was signed up as a fashion columnist in *New!*, which, funnily enough, was the same magazine where Jordan's husband, Peter Andre, had a column. Chantelle was also named the second-happiest woman in Britain in a survey carried out by the *Independent on Sunday*, because she was 'living the dream'. Prince Charles's new wife, the Duchess of Cornwall, came top.

But not everyone was completely enamoured of the new star. A rare moment of bad publicity occurred when Chantelle, who had been booked to appear at an Edinburgh club, was booed off the stage. It is difficult to know exactly what happened, but it appears that she might have let everything go to her head, first refusing to use the club's main entrance and then threatening to leave if she was asked any difficult questions. When she appeared on stage, she was pelted with plastic cups and so left early anyway.

'Chantelle was a complete nightmare from the off,' said an insider. 'The club have had Justin Timberlake and Christina Aguilera through the doors in the past and they weren't half as much of a handful as Chantelle.'

It was perhaps an early warning that Chantelle must guard against it all going to her head, although, that said, it might well have been a mistaken report. Some people who had been at the club spoke up to say that nothing had been thrown and that Chantelle had a whale of a time.

All the accoutrements of celebrity began to

appear. Websites sprang up, completely devoted to Chantelle. Soon her fame was such that she was routinely discussed by other celebrities: for example, when Molly of Daft Fader was asked whether she'd rather go on *Who Wants To Be A Millionaire* with Chantelle or Jade Goody, she replied, 'Oh, that is a question. Erm... probably Chantelle actually. She is a little bit ditsy, for sure, but she surprised me on *Big Brother*. She knew some stuff that I didn't think she would know.'

Did Molly think Chantelle was pretending to be less intelligent than she actually was? 'Oh, I don't know. I think she was quite genuine. I wouldn't say she was thick. I just think that sometimes she's not really there. But I'm not really there a lot of the time. We'd make a great team.'

Far from making £100,000 after leaving the house, Chantelle looks set to earn at least £1 million and perhaps twice that, depending on what happens to the wedding. There have been magazine articles advising young girls how to make themselves look like Chantelle and any number of reports about her in the gossip columns. And still the interest in her has shown no sign of subsiding at all. She is a heroine for our times – a modern Becky Sharpe.

12

Into the Future

Now that Chantelle and Preston were officially engaged, you could be forgiven for thinking that some of the intense interest surrounding them would fade away. Not a bit of it. Quite apart from a fresh bout of speculation as to where the wedding was going to be, who would be attending and what would happen next, every word that the happy couple spoke was weighed up and scrutinised.

Throughout it all, they appeared to cope remarkably well. She might not have been accustomed to media attention in the pre-*Big Brother* days, but Chantelle was coping with it extraordinarily well now. So adept was she at coping with all the attention and aggravation that, to anyone who didn't know her story, she would have come across as an old hand.

The world of commerce was not slow to get in on the celebrations. The sweets manufacturer Haribo promptly designed a huge box of goodies, emblazoned with a picture of the couple in the middle of a giant heart and bearing the message 'A tub of love wishing you the sweetest engagement ever'. A spokesperson for the company said, 'We wanted to produce the sweetest of gifts for Chantelle and Preston to celebrate their very happy engagement. It's the perfect romantic treat for the pair to cuddle up and share. We wish them both a lifetime of happiness together.' It was a move that caught the public's imagination, especially when rumours circulated that Chantelle wished to keep the box unopened until the romance bore fruit and she and Preston could share it with a third member of the new family. Whether this was true or not was neither here nor there.

Of course, there was a little explaining to be done, too. Cynics were quick to point out that this was the second time Preston had got engaged in three months; so much so that the man himself decided to put forward his side of the story. 'I just panicked and wanted to make things right and I had these feelings for Chantelle that I shouldn't have had,' he said. 'In the house, the thought of me with Chantelle didn't enter my mind, because I knew I wasn't allowed to… so I really hadn't thought about it. When I came out of the house, I had a chance to weigh everything up, and I was like, Shit, I really want to make everything right with Camille.

'Like an idiot, I thought that was the right thing to do and I guess it made everything worse – eventually, we had a conversation that led to us splitting up. If people think I'm a shit, that's fine, but I'm happy and madly in love. If that's what I have to deal with in order to be ridiculously happy with the girl that I'm madly in love with, that's OK.'

There was also a certain amount of embarrassment when it emerged that the ring Preston had given to Chantelle was the exact same one with which he became engaged to Camille. 'After breaking off his engagement to Camille, Preston begged her to give him the ring back,' said a source close to the couple. 'She didn't want it if they weren't to be together. Preston is certain Chantelle is "the one" and they can't wait to get married later this year.'

Chantelle was not upset by the news, though. The ring had originally belonged to Preston's great-grandmother, and so was associated with his family rather than anyone else. 'Chantelle loves the ring and thinks it's nice it has a special family meaning,' said the friend. 'She knows he'd given it to Camille. She told her mum and said, "It's cool. I just love the ring."'

Paris Hilton – the original one – was said to be delighted when she found out. It was even said that she was planning a surprise engagement present for them – a weekend in Paris, the city. 'Paris was over the moon to hear Preston had proposed and couldn't wait to send them a gift,' said a friend. 'But what does a girl with everything get them? What better than a top-notch weekend in Paris with her and her boyfriend, Greek shipping heir Stavros Niarchos? She will arrange the trip for the end of July when her work commitments die down. The four of them will eat in all the best restaurants and see all the romantic sights before taking in a night at the Opera Bastille.'

Chantelle's father was also delighted with the news. 'Preston has good intentions,' Alan said. 'There is a chemistry between them and I think it's fabulous news.' In fact, Chantelle's parents have grown happier by the day as they've watched the progress of their much-loved daughter. And the strength of her relationship with the two of them is both a great help in her efforts to stay in touch with some sort of reality, as well as boosting her appeal to the outside world. Chantelle is, at one and the same time, the archetypal girl next door and the one who got lucky.

As for Camille, she took the news of the engagement with remarkable dignity. Some of the savagery that she initially felt seemed to have calmed down, leaving her more bemused than anything else at the turn of events. 'I'm surprised they got together because Chantelle and I are so different,' she said. 'We have different interests, personalities and backgrounds. He loved that I had a politics degree and a master's. We sat for hours discussing politics and the state of the world, and had a real connection. Then he leaves me for someone so different.'

Certainly, Preston and Chantelle came from quite different backgrounds. Chantelle was a typical Essex girl in her tastes and interests. Preston's ancestors included a prime minister, Earl Grey, and his mother's family came from the United States, which had led to him working for a time at the Museum of Modern Art in New York. He had been sent to a private prep school, Sompting Abbots, near Brighton, which charged £9,660 a year, and had enjoyed a very privileged life when growing up. 'My dad came from a really good family,' he said. 'My parents were really middle class – we weren't allowed to watch telly when we had dinner.' Like so many mockney stars who try to play down their backgrounds – think Guy Ritchie – Preston is really quite posh.

When it came to Chantelle, it was certainly a case of opposites attract. But then why shouldn't they? On the evidence to date, Chantelle is far from being the 'blonde bimbo' she describes herself as. She may have left school at 16 and she may not have had intellectual pursuits, but she was not unintelligent. Since linking up with Preston, she had even been seen at art galleries and book awards ceremonies. It was entirely possible the couple would educate each other about their tastes.

But still it was an odd match. Someone else who seemed a little bemused was Jodie Marsh. 'Is it a sham? What do you think?' she asked. 'All I'll say is that they have very clever agents.'

That other amply cleavaged reality-TV girl Jordan appeared to agree. She was not happy about suggestions that Chantelle and Preston were the new Jordan and Peter Andre, and she was sounding decidedly irritable about Chantelle's existence at all. Criticising the two of them for getting engaged after such a short time, she said, 'I just want to say there's no other couple like Pete and me. If anyone else is trying to be like us, they should stop now. They know who they are – Preston and Chantelle. I'm sick to death of reading that they're getting married and there are all these set-up photos of her coming out of a shop with all her shopping bags. It's so boring now. I liked her in the *Big Brother* house, but get a job now. Let's see if you can do something. Bring it on!'

Chantelle had been ruffling feathers from the moment she emerged from the *Big Brother* household among other reality-TV stars who were clearly worried that she was treading on their patch. Reality television may be a fast track to celebrity, but it is not necessarily an enduring one. In fairness, Jordan was more than a reality-television star, having made her name out of her gravity-defying, if surgically enhanced, breasts, but even she got more coverage now because of her personal life. There is, to date, no reality-TV star who has had a longer career than Jade Goody, and she's only been on the scene for four years. It remains to be seen if Chantelle can beat that.

Chantelle herself laughed it off. She didn't respond publicly, but she did allow sources close to her to make her views known. 'They're nothing alike, are they?' said one source. 'Jordan's worked hard to get where she is and Chantelle's life now is a Cinderella dream come true. And Chantelle has worked nonstop since leaving the *Big Brother* house. The whole thing is just a bit unfair.' It was also a little hurtful, given that Chantelle had publicly expressed her admiration for her pneumatic inspiration, but no one said that reality television was fair. Those who had managed to grasp the crown had no intention of relinquishing it.

Some people were certainly changing their view of Chantelle. Her ex-housemate George Galloway, who had given the impression that he thought she was a bit of a dumb blonde, now said she was 'sharp as a tack'. And she is. It has been said before but the point bears repeating: Chantelle went from being a nobody with modest means to a celebrity with a fortune in the bank and a famous fiancé within a matter of months. Anyone who can do that clearly has more to them than just a head of dyed-blonde hair.

And observers were keen to point out quite how much money she and Preston were now making, especially after Chantelle added a contract with Motorola to her portfolio. Together, they stood to make even more. 'It has been proven that contestants who get together post-reality shows make a lot of money – Jordan and Peter Andre being the prime example,' says Mark Borkowski, a celebrity PR. 'As single entities, Chantelle and

Preston were running out of gas. So it was highly likely they'd get their acts together and team up. I wouldn't place any bets on them staying together long term. But at least they would be able to make more money from a divorce.'

Chantelle herself point-blank denied the fact that money played a part in her plans. 'I haven't got pound signs in my eyes,' she said. 'I haven't even thought about the money.' She was, though, beginning to savour the fruits of her success, taking delivery of a new £15,000 Vauxhall Tigra. And, like so many celebrities, she was beginning to discover that the richer you are, the more likely people are to give you things for free. Given how much she was now being photographed, her look was beginning to have an influence on the way that some of her admirers dressed, and there was money in that. It was becoming a distinct benefit to clothing companies to picture her in their finery, and so a great many items of complimentary clothing were finding their way to her door.

Nevertheless, people continued to snipe at Chantelle's success and even the usually mild-mannered Declan Donnelly, one half of Ant and Dec, expressed reservations about her extraordinary rise to fame. 'Chantelle is like a trick played on celebrities that has got out of hand. I'm not sure that would happen in any other country. Celebrity used to be a by-product of your day job, but now it's just a day job to be a celebrity. That never used to exist before. I wonder how many kids now do want to be firemen and policemen and nurses and stuff, and how many kids just want to be famous. It's a sad kind of reflection.'

Ant, at least, was a little less concerned. 'It's no challenge to what I do,' he said. 'If they're in the paper more than me, then that's good. It's very curious, though; it will be interesting to see what happens.'

But, big as she had become, Chantelle was just among the first of a breed of people that would continue to grow in number. Another series of *Celebrity Love Island* was now in the offing and there were plans to put at least two non-celebs within the midst of the famous, in the hope that one or both would turn out to be another Chantelle. 'The bosses saw how well it worked having a nobody in the *Celebrity Big Brother* house and how it turned Chantelle into one of the UK's hottest new stars,' said a source on the show. 'If they pick someone off the street who has the hots for Sophie Anderton and they place them in an exotic setting with their idol, it will make great telly. Celebs usually prefer to date celebs and they may not like the idea of having two "no-marks" on the island with them. They may look on them as intruders.'

All this certainly raised questions about the real nature of fame. Dec was clearly not motivated by envy or a desire to protect his own position: he was making a perfectly valid point. For it must be said that there are many downsides to instant celebrity achieved on the back of very little: some *Big Brother* contestants have spoken of the shock that greeted them when they were back in the real world. Others find the loss of their short-lived celebrity status hard to bear.

There are other pressures: Jade Goody has admitted to an addiction to slimming pills, as a result of trying to stay as slim as the competition, which, of course, includes Chantelle. And, as Dec said, there is the danger that children will aspire to fame just for the sake of it, rather than aiming for any real and relevant goal. Chantelle, although she was almost certainly not aware of it, was taking part in a very strange experiment, the effects of which will only be known over the longer term.

Not that she was concerned about that. As she settled into life with Preston, there were reports that she had banned him from smoking in their home, followed by speculation that she was pregnant after the two were seen looking at baby clothes in the Brighton branch of BHS. 'She seemed interested in the little pink outfits,' said an onlooker. 'I saw them later on in the adult nightwear section. Chantelle was looking at a pair of Winnie the Pooh pyjamas.'

While her agent denied that Chantelle was expecting a child, it was true that the star was keen to do so as quickly as possible. 'There was a photo of me looking a bit pregnant but I'm so not,' Chantelle said. 'I'd probably just eaten a big lunch! Even my mum called me up, going, "You're not, are you?", so I had to convince her I wasn't, but we laugh about it now. But I've read it so many times that I'm beginning to believe it myself! Babies are something I would've definitely said no to six months ago, but my mind has been changed so it's yes now! Ours will probably come out with blonde hair extensions and covered in tattoos!'

She was also a little more forthcoming about their life together. With such busy schedules, they clearly had to spend a lot of time apart, but, she revealed, their mobile phones came in handy. 'We say all sorts of things to each other in texts,' she revealed. As for when they were actually together, 'Yeah, it's intense and passionate in the bedroom. We're just really excited to see one another and like to spend a lot of time alone.'

Every time they spent a lot of time together in public, though, their profiles rocketed in a way that continued to benefit them both. People had been keen to point out that Chantelle was now earning a great deal of money from her fame and popularity, but exactly the same was true of Preston as well. Before *Celebrity Big Brother*, most people had never heard of the Ordinary Boys, whereas now the group had had a Top Ten hit with the re-release of their single 'Boys Will Be Boys', Preston had been DJ-ing on Virgin Radio and, to cap it all, it had just been announced that they would be touring with Robbie Williams in the summer.

Others in the industry remarked on this new round of success for the band. 'I saw them at the South by Southwest festival last year and I thought, This is completely over,' said Conor McNicholas, editor of *NME*. 'If you'd told me last November that we'd have the Ordinary Boys on our cover by February, I'd have laughed at you.' An appearance on reality television was clearly a boost to Preston just as much as it was to his fiancée.

The extent to which the lives of both of them had changed could not have been better illustrated than by reports that Working Title, the company behind *Four Weddings and a Funeral* and a good deal else, was interested in making a film starring the couple. It would be made in Hollywood and there were already talks about the plot.

'Chantelle and Preston have something unique in their pairing in that Preston is this hip singer and Chantelle a down-to-earth model,' said an insider. 'The idea Working Title want to run with is a storyline based on two people falling for one another on a reality-TV show. It would then trail the twists and turns of the couple throughout their lives. In the film script, it is Chantelle's career which eventually overtakes Preston's and people will see how the couple will cope with that. And it will be a very bumpy ride. At the moment, Chantelle's character is based on her characteristics and looks but the female lead will be given a different name.

'Preston's character will also be similar to him. But movie bosses in America may change him from being a Britpop mod star to a rap star because of the market to which they will be pitching it. Chantelle herself would be quite something if she visited Los Angeles. She's so quirky and different. Despite being blonde and someone who could be mistaken for your average Californian girl, she oozes something unique. And the people there will go mad for her British accent and her eccentric ways.'

And, of course, there was now the wedding to plan. There seemed no reason to hang about, and so the duo decided on late summer. 'We're thinking about a big country manor house at the end of

August or start of September because neither of us are religious,' Chantelle said. 'I just want people there who I've spoken to in the last five years at least and who are a big part of my life. I absolutely hate weddings where you have to ask people what they've been up to – I should already know! Since *Celebrity Big Brother*, I've had people saying they're my best mates, but I think, Why haven't they said that to me instead of telling a magazine?'

Actually, by showbiz standards, their wedding was actually going to be pretty discreet. After a cancellation at the Stock Brook Country Club in Essex for a date in August, the couple stepped in to claim the slot as their own. But it was not an ostentatious place: there was to be room for just 250 people and the deposit was only £3,000. That said, it was an elegant location. 'Chantelle wanted class and was thrilled when the booking became available,' said a source close to the pair. 'She is getting used to the finer things in life and this place delivers.'

Nor did Chantelle appear to be going over the top in her choice of wedding dress. The couple were spotted looking at dresses in Pronuptia in Hove, close to where they lived. 'They looked sweet together,' said the assistant. 'Really happy and really in love.'

And initially they didn't look likely to follow the

example of Jordan and Peter by selling their nuptials to a magazine. This decision, of course, was not set in stone, but Preston was reluctant to do so, not least because the Ordinary Boys were an indie band and he didn't want to do anything that might make them look naff. 'Preston is really pleased with how things with the band are going and he doesn't want to jeopardise that,' said a friend. 'He thinks by selling the rights to his big day he'll lose credibility among the trendy indie crowd.'

His band mates tended to agree. 'We want to be respected for our music, not because our singer is on TV having a drunken fumble with a blonde,' said James Gregory, the group's bassist.

However, shortly afterwards, reports began to circulate that *OK!* was willing to put a deal worth £1 million plus on the table – and possibly even one that would exceed the record-breaking £2 million that Jordan and Peter had been paid. The opportunity suddenly began to look a little bit more attractive than it had before. 'Chantelle thinks it's funny they are in the same ballpark,' said a friend, and she could be forgiven for thinking just that.

In fact, Chantelle could be forgiven for being point-blank amazed at everything that has happened for her in 2006. Even ten years ago, there was no one like Chantelle – not in terms of personality, for Essex blondes are nothing new, but in terms of the nature of her celebrity. She is simply famous for being famous, with no more reason to it than that. Even the likes of Tara Palmer-Tomkinson, who was a sort of precursor to Chantelle and the current generation of reality-television stars, had some nebulous reason for being propelled into the limelight to begin with, in her case a family connection to Prince Charles.

But Chantelle had none of that – which is itself one of the reasons for her massive popularity. She arose from complete obscurity to become famous, literally overnight. And fame is what so many people aspire to today. It is almost as if a person's existence can't be validated unless the whole world knows about it. Now that almost everyone in the country knows about Chantelle, it means, quite simply, that there is a new purpose to her life.

Another aspect of life for reality-TV stars is that they make a huge amount of money simply for being themselves. And for Chantelle, apart from the presenting and promotional work, paid-for interviews with magazines about where her life with Preston is now are a staple form of income. Whatever happens next between them – marriage or a split, children or a new career direction – will be news and they will get paid for talking about it. If they do happen to split, and at the time of writing there is no suggestion of that, then that will be big news itself.

It is impossible to say whether her new life will make Chantelle happy in the longer term. Fame can have a huge downside, especially when things go wrong, and, without a basis of any actual achievement behind her, she might find it difficult to cope. She might also find it difficult if her newfound celebrity disappears. On the plus side, she has the advantage of a very solid home life behind her: she is close to both her parents and has plenty of people to fall back on if problems do arise.

But perhaps they won't. Chantelle, Jade and the lot of them are a new breed of person, a new type of celebrity, and it is up to them to make up the rules as they go along. These are people who have taken what life has given them and made the best of it, in some cases with spectacular results. And if these women are careful – and, curiously, quite a few of these reality stars are women – they will be set up for life.

A few years from now, Chantelle might just be a distant memory in the national consciousness of a pretty blonde who once starred in a television show, but the lady herself, if she is sensible, should be doing just fine. This is Chantelle's moment, and with it the moment of everyone who yearns to step out of their mundane life and into a new and glamorous realm. Chantelle said it herself: she is living the dream. And who could begrudge her that?